MANAGING PERSONAL LEARNING AND CHANGE

THE BUSINESS OF TRAINING
Achieving Success in Changing World Markets
Trevor Bentley   ISBN 0-07-707328-2

EVALUATING TRAINING EFFECTIVENESS
Translating Theory into Practice
Peter Bramley   ISBN 0-07-707331-2

MAKING MANAGEMENT DEVELOPMENT WORK
Achieving Success in the Nineties
Charles Margerison   ISBN 0-07-707382-7

DEVELOPING EFFECTIVE TRAINING SKILLS
Tony Pont   ISBN 0-07-707383-5

HOW TO DESIGN EFFECTIVE TEXT-BASED OPEN
LEARNING: A Modular Course
Nigel Harrison   ISBN 0-07-707355-X

HOW TO DESIGN EFFECTIVE COMPUTER BASED
TRAINING: A Modular Course
Nigel Harrison   ISBN 0-07-707354-1

Details of these and other titles in the series are available from:

The Product Manager, Professional Books, McGraw-Hill Book Company (UK)
Limited, Shoppenhangers Road, Maidenhead, Berkshire, SL6 2QL.
Telephone 0628 23432 Fax 0628 770224

Managing personal learning and change

A trainer's guide

Neil Clark

McGRAW-HILL BOOK COMPANY

London · New York · St Louis · San Francisco · Auckland
Bogotá · Caracas · Hamburg · Lisbon · Madrid · Mexico · Milan
Montreal · New Delhi · Panama · Paris · San Juan · São Paulo
Singapore · Sydney · Tokyo · Toronto

Published by
McGRAW-HILL Book Company (UK) Limited
Shoppenhangers Road, Maidenhead, Berkshire, SL6 2QL, England.
Telephone 0628 23432
Fax 0628 770224

British Library Cataloguing in Publication Data
Clark, Neil
    Managing personal learning and change.
    1. Personal. Training.
    I. Title
    658.3124

    ISBN 0-07-707344-4

Library of Congress Cataloging-in-Publication Data
Clark, Neil
    Managing personal learning and change: a trainers guide/Neil
Clark.
        p.   cm. — (The McGraw-Hill training series)
    Includes bibliographical references and index.
    ISBN 0-07-707344-4
    1. Employees—Training of.   I. Title.   II. Series.
HF5549.5.T7C588   1990
658.3'12404—dc20   90-44670

12345 BP 94321

Typeset by Book Ens Limited, Baldock, Herts
and printed and bound in Great Britain by The Bath Press, Avon

Contents

Series preface

Training and development are now firmly centre stage in most organizations, if not all. Nothing unusual in that—for some organizations. They have always seen training and development as part of the heart of their businesses. More and more must see it the same way.

The pressure is on for them to do so. This pressure is coming from varied sources. The government, the CBI, the unions, the BIM, the new TECs, the EC and foreign competition are all exerting pressure—not just for more training, but for more relevant, appropriate and useful training.

In addition, the demographic trends through the nineties will inject into the marketplace severe competition for good people who will need good training. Young people without conventional qualifications, skilled workers in redundant crafts, people out of work, women wishing to return to work—all will require excellent training to fit them to meet the job demands of the 1990s and beyond.

But excellent training does not spring from what we have done well in the past. T&D specialists are in a new ball game. 'Maintenance' training—training to keep up skill levels to do what we have always done—will be less in demand. Rather, organization, work and market change training are now much more important and will remain so for some time. Changing organizations and people is no easy task, requiring special skills and expertise which, sadly, many T&D specialists do not possess.

To work as a 'change' specialist requires us to get to centre stage—to the heart of the company's business. This means we have to ask about future goals and strategies and even be involved in their development, at least as far as T&D policies are concerned.

This demands excellent communication skills, political expertise, negotiating ability, diagnostic skills—indeed, all the skills a good internal consultant requires.

The implications for T&D specialists are considerable. It is not enough merely to be skilled in the basics of training, we must also begin to act like business people and to think in business terms and talk the language of business. We must be able to resource training not just from within but by using the vast array of external resources. We must be able to manage our activities as well as any other manager. We must share in the creation and communication of the company's vision. We must never let the goals of the company out of our sight.

In short, we may have to grow and change with the business. It will be hard. We shall not only have to demonstrate relevance but also value for money and achievement of results. We shall be our own boss, as accountable for results as any other line manager, and we shall have to deal with fewer internal resources.

The challenge is on, as many T&D specialists have demonstrated to me over the past few years. We need to be capable of meeting that challenge. This is why McGraw-Hill Book Company (UK) Limited have planned and launched this major new training series—to help us meet that challenge.

The series covers all aspects of T&D and provides the knowledge base from which we can develop plans to meet the challenge. They are practical books for the professional person. They are a starting point for planning our journey into the twenty-first century.

Use them well. Don't just read them. Highlight key ideas, thoughts, action pointers or whatever, and have a go at doing something with them. Through experimentation we evolve; through stagnation we die.

I know that all the authors in the McGraw-Hill Training Series would want me to wish you good luck. Have a great journey into the twenty-first century.

ROGER BENNETT
Series Editor

About the series editor

Roger Bennett has over twenty years' experience in training, management education, research and consulting. He has long been involved with trainer training. He has carried out research into trainer effectiveness and conducted workshops, seminars and conferences on the subject around the world. He has written extensively on the subject including the book *Improving Trainer Effectiveness*, Gower. His work has also taken him all over the world and has involved directors of companies as well as managers and trainers.

Roger Bennett has worked in engineering, several business schools (including the International Management Centre, where he launched the UK's first masters degree in T&D) and has been a board director of two companies. He is the editor of the *Journal of European Industrial Training* and was series editor of the ITD's *Get In There* workbook and video package for the managers of training departments. He now runs his own business called The Management Development Consultancy.

Preface

During the writing of this book I have, on many occasions, been aware of a number of people who have significantly influenced the ideas, approaches and practices that I have described. Without wishing to associate these individuals with any of the views expressed—as always, they will exercise their own judgement—I would like to take this opportunity publicly to acknowledge my appreciation of their contribution.

In chronological order I wish to thank:

John Sutcliffe (for sharing his skills in, and enthusiasm for, counselling);
Tony Fraser (for introducing me to Gestalt and helping me realize that the trainer has to discover a personal style);
Keri Phillips (for that period of co-training when we created and provided so many successful programmes);
Robin Evenden (for helping me appreciate that the trainer has a true professional responsibility to both the learner and the client organization);
Hilda Courtney (for introducing me to Gestalt therapy and helping me to learn);
Gary Yontef (for his explication of, and enthusiasm for, Gestalt theory);
Bob and Rita Resnick (for demonstrating that Gestalt therapy can be both powerful and caring);
Ian McMonogale (for our discussions on counselling and his comments on some of the text);
Peter Murray (for our discussions on consultancy and his comments on the text).

I would also like to acknowledge my gratitude to W H Smith Ltd, the London Borough of Hammersmith and Fulham Housing Department, the Milk Marketing Board, Sherratt & Hughes, and the Architect's Department of Newcastle City Council, for their permission to allow me to publish descriptions of learning activities that I have provided for them.

Finally, and most significantly, I would like to acknowledge that without the support of my wife, Sylvia, and our children, Simon, Iain, and Jenny, this book, and what it represents would not have been produced.

April 1990

Introduction

This book is aimed at the training practitioner working within an organization, who is providing, or attempting to provide, the normal range of training and development services. There is no expectation that such a reader will bring to this book any particular skills or knowledge about training, learning theory, or psychotherapy. There is an expectation, however, that the reader has experience of attempting to help others learn and change through the medium of training, counselling, or consultancy. For such a reader will be bringing to this book a number of questions, ideas and thoughts about the practical difficulties involved in attempting to carry out such tasks. He or she will also be bringing a number of concerns about their adequacy and ability to offer such a service. If you have no such concerns about your ability then this book has little to offer.

Having been a trainer for 16 years—within an organization, at a management college, and, latterly, as an independent consultant—I am ruefully aware that much of my understanding and skills derive from my practical experience and owe little to either the literature on training or to my attendance on training of trainers programmes. This statement is not intended to be a casual dismissal of either the literature or the courses that I have attended. Rather, it is a simple recognition that the issues that most concerned me as a trainer were not addressed, and that both the courses and the literature looked at training as a technical activity requiring mechanistic solutions. It was many years before I realized that other trainers, like myself, felt nervous and anxious before events; that they also dreaded the prospect of once more encountering the 'difficult' course member or the 'difficult' group; that they also experienced times when they did not know what to do or say; and that they also had doubts about their abilities and capacity to manage learning events. It is true that a number of them have attempted to resolve such doubts by subscribing totally to the concept of non-directive learning. The *reductio ad absurdum* of this concept is that not only do individuals know what they need to learn but also know how they need to learn. This has always struck me as being an unhappy partner to the well-known thesis of probability that if an infinite number of chimpanzees were left with typewriters for an unspecified period then they would produce the collected works of Shakespeare.

After the liberation of discovering that other trainers shared my concerns I managed to identify the area of understanding that was missing in my formal development as a trainer. Both the literature that I had read and the courses that I had attended seemed to approach training from either the academic end (e.g. learning theory) or from the mechanistic (e.g. Pfeiffer and Jones[1]). What seemed to be missing—squeezed from both sides as it were—was the simple acknowledgement that fundamental to the role of the trainer was a responsibility for changing the attitudes and behaviours of people, and that this process was a dynamic one involving the trainer as a person and not as a technician.

This responsibility, both challenging and rewarding, is what actually creates the self-doubts and anxieties mentioned above. For what every trainer knows from experience is that the technical elements of the task—understanding the theory inputs, preparing the material, and designing the structure—can soon become routine and undemanding. But the success of the event, however, will be largely determined by the trainer's ability to persuade, cajole or somehow influence this particular group of people to acquire these particular skills, attitudes, or elements of knowledge which have been deemed appropriate or relevant to their job needs. This task is made more difficult by the reality of every training group comprising those who have been forced to attend; those who have been 'diagnosed' as in need of remedial treatment; those who have come with an 'open' mind (i.e. need to be persuaded that the programme has any value); the cynical; the scared; and those who intend to do as little as possible. In many cases, those who actually want to learn and be different, can form a small minority of any group.

This reality helps put into some perspective the orthodox model of training:

> clearly identify the training need +
> provide an appropriate learning experience +
> apply learning to work situation
>
> =
>
> effective and efficient training

The important variable missing from this model is the trainee's willingness or ability to learn and change. Certainly one of the assumptions that I made as a trainer (an assumption policed by those who pay the bill for training) was that if training did not work then it was largely my responsibility as the expert. One symptom of the pressure caused by this responsibility is the obsessive concern trainers have in 'fine-tuning' a particular programme (rewriting handouts or briefs for exercises, adjusting the sequence or timing of sessions etc.—such behaviours reflecting the impossible pursuit of perfection: designing the infallible programme).

I gained a greater understanding of these issues when I started designing and running programmes for trainers at a management college. Within the space of a six-month period I was approached by three organizations to design and run a programme for a group of trainers working within the organization. The commonality of these three requests was to identify and develop the necessary interventions to help individuals and groups to learn and change. The programme which emerged, and which is still run at the college, also led to writing the book *Unfinished Business: The Theory and Practice of Personal Process Work*.[2] Not surprisingly, in retrospect, the search for understanding as reflected in both the programme and the book concentrated on identifying some general principles (e.g. the nature and type of process intervention) and how to apply them. Although, in the spirit of humanism, there was a deliberate avoidance of answers and prescription, the theme of trainer as technician is evident. The dynamic process of personal change arising from the interaction between trainer and course member is implied but not fully explored. Since that book was published in 1984 I have consciously applied myself to the task of looking at that relationship.

Like many of my contemporaries I have looked for assistance in developing my skills and understanding of training in the related area of psychotherapy. Psychotherapy, unlike training, has always addressed itself directly to the processes involved in changing attitudes and behaviours. It has also, from Freud onwards, seen the relationship between the helper (the analyst) and the learner (the patient) as the vehicle for learning. Therefore, it provides a body of knowledge and experience which should be of direct assistance to any trainer. Having made this statement I am aware that linking training with psychotherapy tends to raise hackles, particularly in organizations, and that these emotional responses obscure rather than illuminate some important questions that need to be addressed. (For example, should trainers claim and use an expertise and knowledge when they have no training or qualifications in that area?) For the moment I want to put the questions to one side, and to comment on what trainers have and are still doing in this area.

Since the late 1950s in the UK, trainers have been drawing liberally from the world of psychotherapy. There are two main reasons for this borrowing. First, psychotherapy offers models, theories and techniques which can, and have been applied in the training room. Looking back, it is possible to distinguish a chronological record of this activity—which includes T-groups, Encounter groups, Transactional Analysis, Behaviour Modification, Gestalt, Neuro-Linguistic Programming, Eriksonian hypnotherapy. This record can be traced in the annual handbooks of Pfeiffer and Jones.[3] Because of organizational concerns many trainers have felt the need to take a subversive approach in using this material, and have demonstrated that by reducing this body of knowledge to a set of techniques or simplified ideas. One result is that their activities in this area have meant that these 'experiments' have been used inappropriately and often to the detriment of the needs of both the individuals on the receiving end and their organizations. But this subversion continues.

The second reason for trainers entering the world of psychotherapy— and in my judgement a more important reason—is the valid proposition that in order to help other people change and learn you need first to discover how *you* learn and change. Of equal importance, is the need to understand the myriad of ways in which *you stop* yourself from learning.

Such an experience and understanding not only helps trainers to work through their own particular doubts and anxieties about undertaking the role of the trainer, but also provides a perspective—both theoretical and practical— about designing and providing learning events for others. *The purpose of entering therapy is not for trainers to become therapists or to introduce therapy into an organizational setting.*

Which brings me back to the questions about the relationship between training and therapy and the justifiable concerns of attempting to blend the two approaches. Before identifying some important differences between the two, it is worth looking at what they have in common. First, they are both concerned with helping individuals to learn and change their levels of skill, knowledge and attitudes. In these terms they are both educational processes. Second, they are both concerned with problem-solving, i.e. how to deal with specific situations. Third, they are both concerned with improving an individual's ability to manage uncertainty and new situations. There are also some crucial differences:

1 Therapy is concerned with bringing to the surface historical experiences which are affecting the person's ability to deal with the present.
2 In a therapeutic setting the therapist is attempting to bring the patient to an impasse at which he or she is likely to experience a crisis of choice. At such times the person will experience intense vulnerability, and will need appropriate support.
3 The problems that the person looks at in therapy go much wider than the work situation.
4 For all these reasons therapy requires a long-term professional supporting relationship.

On these grounds, if no other, it is possible for any trainer to be able to draw a clear boundary between training and therapy in all aspects of his or her work.

Like many of my contemporaries I have experienced, at a number of levels, all the approaches to psychotherapy mentioned above. In my own case, I have specialized in Gestalt therapy and have been actively involved in translating my knowledge and experience into the design and provision of learning events in organizations for the last ten years. For me, the particular virtue of Gestalt, which reflects its origins in the work of early Gestalt psychologists, is that it offers more to our understanding of the process of personal learning and change than any other comparable body of theory. Alongside this development of my own understanding, I have had the opportunity and support to apply this perspective in a variety of organizations in an open, rather than subversive, way.

This understanding and experience is what informs the content and structure of this book. Therefore, Chapter 1 looks in detail at the processes involved in personal learning and change. It draws on the model of Gestalt therapy to look at the practical decisions facing the trainer when managing a learning event. Chapter 2 examines the role and responsibilities of the trainer as change agent, in particular at the nature and development of what I have described as the helping relationship. The following three chapters (3, 4 and 5) look at training, counselling and consultancy as the three major vehicles for developing change in organizations. Each chapter will end with practical examples drawn from my experiences in these three areas. Finally, Chapter 6 will examine the experience of being a trainer, and at the problems and opportunities created by the responsibility of helping others to change.

One final comment about the approach adopted in this book. Apart from some concepts from Gestalt used and explained in the first two chapters, I have chosen to limit the amount of theory to a minimum, and have chosen, instead, to draw on my experience of designing and managing learning events.

References

1. J. William Pfeiffer and John E. Jones, *A Handbook of Structured Experiences Vols I–VIII* (University Associates, 1972–9): an Annual handbook for group facilitators.
2. Neil Clark, Keri Phillips and Dave Barker, *Unfinished Business: The Theory and Practice of Personal Process Work* (Gower Press, 1984).
3. Pfieffer *et al.*, *A Handbook of Structured Experiences*.

1 Personal change

It has been a traditional approach within training to distinguish attempts to change knowledge, skills and attitudes. Each of these areas, so the orthodox view asserts, involves different kinds of learning and, therefore, requires different approaches to training. While recognizing the validity of this distinction, and the real differences between, for example, the task of helping people understand current legislation on health and safety at work, as opposed to developing non-racist attitudes, I am choosing to see personal change as embracing any change in knowledge (i.e. information, theory, understanding), in skills (including any kind of behaviour change), or attitudes (to others or self). In spite of the acknowledged differences the process of learning and change is common to all three. For reasons which will become clearer in this chapter I believe such a distinction has become unhelpful. As a learner, rather than as a trainer, such a distinction has not been meaningful for me. For example, on the receiving end of a lecture I know that my capacity to learn that material will be significantly determined by a number of factors—not least by my attitudes to the subject and the presenter, and by my emotional responses to what is happening at the time. In short, I believe that effective learning, of whatever kind, is an experience that should engage the whole person. This view could well be described as the holistic concept of learning.

Within the last ten years there has been a resurgence of interest in the process of learning and much of that has focused on the identification of learning styles. (For example, the initial work of Kolb[1] and Honey and Mumford[2].) One of the consequences of this work appears to be, apart from enthusiastic support from a number of trainers, an encouragement not only to distinguish between the approaches of individuals to learning, but also an encouragement for individuals to adopt a fragmented (i.e. non-holistic) view about their own process of learning. For example, as someone who has been diagnosed as having a dominant learning style of active experimentation, I know even while engaged in experimentation that I am also reflecting and conceptualizing at the same time—in fact, I need to do the latter two things in order to experiment.

As a recent convert to the use of word processors my approach to that particular learning obstacle was to read a few paragraphs of the imposing manual and then simply to start pushing buttons to discover how to use the machine. While pushing the buttons I was reflecting ('Why has the screen gone blank?'), and also conceptualizing ('I should not push that button if I want the text to stay on the screen'). At the same time I was trying to cope with a severe attitude problem ('This proves that I can't cope with modern technology'). My learning process was also clearly shaped by a bewildering array of emotional responses—including rage, frustration, impatience, confusion, anxiety and satisfaction. The fact that in this case I was also highly motivated to learn was a questionable asset. My impatience to master the machine actually hindered my progress.

What did I learn about my process of learning in mastering the word processor? (1), that my attitude concerning my ability to cope with technology was a major determinant of how well I dealt with the task. (2), that my moment-by-moment feelings guided many of my steps in the process. (3), that given a choice between reading the manual or pressing buttons I eschew the former. (4), that my preference is to form concepts based on direct experience rather than on translating someone else's concepts into experience. What conclusions can I as a trainer make about me as a learner acquiring specific skills? That I need to become more aware of how specific feelings and attitudes interrupt or facilitate my learning. This is a different diagnosis from what a trainer with a learning-styles perspective would make of this experience. Such a trainer would be likely to diagnose or assume that I need to develop my capacity to reflect or to conceptualize.

This difference in diagnosis reflects also the difference between the holistic view of learning (paying attention to me as a whole person) and a fragmented view (I need to separate out and focus on discrete aspects of myself).

Learning difficulties

One of the first areas that trainers become aware of is not *how* people learn but the multitude of ways in which they seem unable to learn. The reasons for this emphasis on the negative is simple to explain. First, learning difficulties are easier to see, and if you do have any doubt the learner will make it obvious even if he or she does not state it clearly. Second, most new trainers do have a tendency to look for examples of their failure to be effective, and choose to see all learning difficulties as clearly the trainer's responsibility. (More experienced trainers are likely, by contrast, to blame everyone else for the difficulty rather than themselves. But that is another story!) By studying such examples it does actually help us to understand what learning involves.

The first event I worked on as a trainer—albeit as an assistant to an experienced colleague—was a fairly conventional three-day programme on recruitment skills. The first day and a half was devoted to examining the stages of the recruitment process, looking at interviewing skills, and the particular problems of using a selection panel. The teaching methods used were a mixture of lectures, small-group discussions and skill exercises, and a commercial film illustrating some key points about good practice. The second half of the programme offered all participants an opportunity to conduct simulated interviews, with local schoolchildren acting as candidates. These interviews were filmed on CCTV with other participants acting as observers.

One incident from that programme has stayed with me ever since and has, at different times, provided me with puzzlement, disbelief, amusement and concern. It has only been in the last few years that I have been able to make sense of what occurred.

The incident took place within two minutes of the first role-play that I was responsible for reviewing, and involved the chairperson of the panel asking the candidate, 'Why did you fail "O" level mathematics?' This question produced a tremor of disbelief among the observers, and they made a note of it for the review session. When the feedback was offered, and it was given tactfully, the role players were surprised that it seemed worth mentioning. Even after watching the incident on CCTV they remained puzzled. When the candidate described his response to the question, and said that he felt uncomfortable and disapproved of, their view was that this was a legitimate request for information, and as such was an open and not a judgemental question. They were aware of the difference between the types of question and were able to offer examples of both. This, they concluded, had been a genuine request for important information. At which point both I and the observers retired dumbfounded.

Even I, a novice trainer, could judge that their response to the feedback was genuine rather than defensive. Nor could the three people on the panel be described as either stupid or insensitive. There appeared to be no obvious reason for this divergence of view. The three people wanted to learn, they felt comfortable in the group, with each other, and they accepted all the other feedback. So what was the learning difficulty?

Obviously, my own view is just that—an interpretation—when the true reason can only be provided by the three people concerned. But having experienced similar kinds of learning difficulties myself, and having spoken to others about their experiences, it is possible to speculate that the particular difficulty on this occasion was their lack of awareness about the judgemental part of themselves. Cognitively, they could detect the judgemental aspects of others, but both emotionally as well as cognitively they could not fully recognize that part of themselves. Therefore, the feedback they received was meaningless and in that respect the training event was a failure. In order to analyse this failure more effectively there is a need to step back and see what Gestalt has to say about how people learn.

Gestalt therapy

The contribution of Gestalt psychology to the development of the psychotherapeutic approach of Fritz Perls, among others, is not always clearly acknowledged or explained. This omission is important for two reasons. First, the theoretical basis of the therapy model is impoverished by its absence. Second, the particular contribution of the Gestalt psychologists offers trainers a different perspective on the process of learning.

The birthdate of Gestalt psychology is traditionally placed at 1912. It was in that year that Max Wertheimer, assisted by Kurt Koffka and Wolfgang Kohler, conducted his experiments on perceived motion. The initial concern of this group was to study the nature of perception, but it proved to be an easy step to move from perception to a study of learning. Some key ideas from their work have been described by Edward W. L. Smith:

Based on his careful phenomenological studies of problem solving, Kohler concluded that the problem of learning is secondary to the problem of perception, for the key to learning is the discovery of the right response, which is dependent upon the 'structuring of the field' or Gestalt formation. When one has created the Gestalt, one experiences sudden 'Einsicht' or insight, one's awareness is elevated to a new level, one understands. That sudden moment of insight may come like a flash, with a sense of 'aha!' True insight, the proof positive of learning, is characterised by reproducibility of the behaviour and applicability to new situations. That is if one has learned a new behaviour, one can repeat that behaviour at a future time and can apply that behaviour to other situations which are not identical to the original situation in which the learning occurred.'[3]

Central to their work is the concept of the gestalt, which is a word not easily translated into English. The nearest we can get to its meaning is: whole, configuration, integration, a unique patterning. What it describes is the innate tendency that we all have to structure our perceptions in such a way that we can see the whole picture. For example, on being confronted with the pattern in Figure 1.1 we are likely to see not just a random series of dots but the outline of a circle. If we cannot impose a gestalt on the information and achieve some kind of closure, or understanding, then we either discard the information or feel dissatisfied with the outcome. This helps us to understand one common response to any kind of new situation—for example, avant garde art or music—when our difficulty of discovering a meaningful gestalt could leave us feeling scornful or irritated by what we experience.

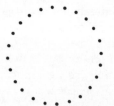

Figure 1.1   *Random dots or circle: forming gestalts*

This process of gestalt formation is a moment by moment experience. So, for example, I write these words to form the gestalt of a sentence which conveys the meaning that I am trying to express. If I am dissatisfied with the result I will rewrite the sentence. When I am satisfied I will be able to move on to the next sentence or idea. If I approached writing in a fragmented way (word by word) rather than in terms of the gestalts of sentences, paragraphs and chapters then the task of writing would be infinitely more difficult than I experience at the moment.

Some of the other important concepts from Gestalt psychology that Perls borrowed were: unfinished situation and figure/ground. The first

of these I have already alluded to. An unfinished situation arises whenever we are unable to complete the gestalt and we are left with some
level of dissatisfaction. An everyday example of this is when we are presented with a puzzle of some sort, e.g. crossword, jigsaw, Rubik's cube,
that we just cannot solve. At such a point the level of dissatisfaction is
so acute that we feel unable to move on to something else and the nag-
ging problem stays in our mind. It seems that our capacity to store such
unfinished situations is quite profound but though the initial level of
irritation dies away each unfinished situation does accumulate further
dissatisfaction. Over time this level of dissatisfaction actively interferes
with our ability to deal with similar tasks. So for instance, my difficulty
in learning how to manage the word processor was influenced by similar experiences of dealing with technology (in my case anything more
complex than a fountain pen) and many of the emotional responses that
I mentioned were 'replays' of those events. Hence, my attitude problem
about my ability to cope.

The figure/ground concept describes the process involved in structuring
perceptions. At each moment there is an infinite number of features that
I can pay attention to (the keyboard, my immediate surroundings,
thoughts, feelings, memories, the sights and sounds of the external
world etc.). This vast range of possibilities is designated as the 'ground'.
But, moment by moment, I am choosing a 'figure' of interest from this
range of choice. For the last thirty seconds it was the sounds outside my
window—a welcome break from writing. The figure emerges and
becomes a gestalt (in this case for relaxation) and then drops away to
allow another gestalt to emerge. There is a well-known illustration of
the old/young woman which demonstrates this process. With the same
illustration the figure that emerges for some people is the face of an old
crone, while for others they see the face of a beautiful young woman.

This stage of developing the figure from the ground is an area that Perls
was to examine in some detail. For the moment I will give a further
example of this process based on my experiences of being a trainer. In
my early days as a trainer, an older and more experienced colleague
told me that in every training group there is always one troublemaker
who needed to be dealt with. He was right! Week in and week out I
would find one troublemaker in every group. Then another colleague
with whom I worked asked me why I kept picking fights with at least
one person in every group. Since that question there seems to have
been a profound change in the nature of the groups with which I work!

Frederick S. Perls (1893–1970), now recognized as the founder of
Gestalt therapy, began to apply these ideas in the field of psychotherapy
in the 1940s. 'Fritz' Perls originally qualified as a doctor in Berlin in
1921. He was trained in psychoanalysis at the Psychoanalytical Institutes
of Berlin, Frankfurt and Vienna. During his time at Frankfurt Perls
became acquainted with the work of the Gestalt psychologists, particularly Max Wertheimer and Wolfgang Kohler. Although he later
described himself as 'not a pure Gestaltist',[4] Perls was particularly interested in the idea of the unfinished situation, the incomplete gestalt.
Forced to flee Germany with his wife, Laura, he worked in private practice
in Amsterdam in 1933–34, until the threat of Nazism made it necessary

to emigrate to South Africa, where he became a training psychoanalyst, served as a psychiatrist for the British Army, and established the South Africa Institute for Psychoanalysis in 1935. In 1942 he published *Ego, Hunger and Aggression*[5] which was his first attempt to describe what he was calling then 'concentration therapy'. In 1946 he moved to the United States where he worked in private practice, and later became psychiatrist in residence at Esalen Institute, Big Sur, California, where he conducted training workshops and seminars in Gestalt therapy from 1964 to 1969. The term 'Gestalt therapy' was first used as a title of a book on Perls's methods, written by him and co-authors Ralph Hefferline and Paul Goodman in 1951.[6] Before his death Perls founded, or helped to establish, the Institute for Gestalt Therapy in New York, and similar institutes in Cleveland and San Francisco.

Although in the later years, and since, Perls and his early followers adopted a provocatively anti-intellectual and over-simplified approach in their practice of Gestalt, he, along with a number of important contributors, had successfully established the theoretical base of Gestalt therapy. In the last ten years there have been significant attempts by a number of reputable institutions, including the Gestalt Institutes in Los Angeles and Cleveland, to build upon the theoretical base. This has involved moving away from the practices and approach used by Perls in the last ten years of his life, and not only going back to his earlier contributions but also acknowledging those made by his contemporaries, not least the contribution of his wife, Laura.[7]

Gestalt formation and destruction

Perls's development of some of the ideas of Gestalt psychology came from his attempt to develop the theoretical base of psychoanalysis. His work with Laura in describing the gratification of the hunger instinct (*Ego, Hunger and Aggression*) as a driving force in personality development led him to apply the model of gestalt formation and destruction to the wider process of need satisfaction. His basic premise was that just as we structure our perceptions through the formation of gestalt figures we similarly organize ourselves in the satisfaction and destruction of the whole realm of physical, emotional and psychological needs. These needs are present in a hierarchy so priorities resulting from the relationship between the individual and the environment are fulfilled to drop away and be replaced by other needs. The cycle of gestalt formation and destruction is diagrammatically shown in Figure 1.2.

The cycle involves starting from a new situation (i.e. open to all the possibilities); at some stage a need will emerge, and the individual will become aware of that need, then organize him- or herself to take appropriate action which will involve making contact with some aspect of the environment. Having satisfied the need the individual is ready to move on to the next need. This period between needs is referred to as *pregnanz*.

An example of this cycle in action could be, for instance, my experience of writing this book. As I continue writing I become aware of a dryness in my throat and I recognize my need to have some liquid refreshment. Once I am aware, I organize myself to take appropriate action—in this

Figure 1.2 *The cycle of gestalt formation and destruction: basic model*

case making a cup of tea. This involves my identifying and 'contacting' different aspects of my environment (teabag, milk, kettle etc.). Having satisfied my thirst I am then able and ready to continue writing.

All those but the mentally or physically sick and the poor or oppressed can orient and organize themselves sufficiently to satisfy their needs concerned with most physical functioning. The majority find breathing, eating, drinking, excreting and resting fairly straightforward and satisfying, although this is not as obvious as it perhaps seems at first glance. People who eat too much or too little, drink too much, suffer from constipation or insomnia are not generally thought of as 'sick', but for each of us at such times even basic physical functioning can present difficulties.

To return to my 'simple' example of thirst, I can interrupt that healthy cycle of need satisfaction at a number of levels. (1), I could be so oblivious of my physical state that my need would have to become chronic (e.g. dehydration) before I became aware of what was happening. (2), I might be aware of the need but decide either to suppress the need (i.e. ignore it) or choose to delay satisfying it on the grounds that I must not interrupt what I am doing. (3), I might have no previous experience of making a cup of tea, and rather than risk experimenting may choose to do nothing. (4), I might not know where the various elements required to make a cup of tea are, and so choose to do nothing. (5), if I do not actually have all the elements in my immediate environment (the house), I may choose to do nothing. Whatever the nature of the particular interruption, if I do not satisfy the need a time will come when my thirst is so figural that it will stop me writing or doing anything else. This state may be described as an unfinished situation, or in Gestalt therapy terms as unfinished business.

The emotional and psychological needs are more elusive. For example, the need to give and receive approval, love, recognition, companionship, stimulation, interest, acceptance and care. In terms of these needs the individual may have problems in perceiving the need clearly or may not know how to satisfy the need. When dealing with these kinds of needs our experience may be a sense of confusion or uneasiness.

An example in management might be an employee's uneasy feeling that her boss treats other members of staff in a more relaxed and informal way. The boss may seem to talk to them frequently, freely and with warmth. But with her the boss is rather formal and more abrupt. She perhaps feels hurt and isolated and finds herself pulling back from contact both with the boss and her peers. This dissatisfaction leads to a sense of isolation, low motivation and a drop in work output which in itself produces a vicious spiral. The employee tells herself there is nothing she can do: either she carries on as she is or she goes and finds herself another job.

Here the need for personal recognition and acceptance remains unsatisfied and being unfinished business disturbs the healthy pattern of emerging needs and their satisfaction. In this way the accumulation of unfinished business impedes the individual so that she becomes less clear and less ready for the next experience.

In terms of the Gestalt model the ground can become overcrowded with urgent unsatisfied needs, each competing with each other for priority. Like a crowd of people trying to get through a narrow doorway at the same time few, if any, actually get through. By contrast, the ground can become impoverished by a habitual denial or repression of needs. If I choose, as I once did, to see only the troublemakers in a training group, then the consequence is that not only am I guaranteed to find such 'figures' but I also do not see more positive kinds of figure, e.g. those aspects of the person that want to learn and change or those people who present no problem.

Interruptions   Gestalt therapy is directly concerned with the ways people interrupt their contact with the environment and avoid the possibility of satisfying their needs at any one time. These interruptions are learned patterns of behaviour which made sense at some stage in our life—usually in the early relationship between the child and the parent—but now are often inappropriate in relationships with others and the world generally. For example, a child who is constantly 'corrected' by parents for being too inquisitive will choose to limit his or her curiosity about people and objects. Over time there is an obvious consequence that the impulse of curiosity will be completely suppressed. The child may develop into an adult who uncritically accepts or rejects whatever is encountered, i.e. the instinct of curiosity appears to be absent. Such early decisions about how to be in the world are 'healthy' adaptations to a particular environment, e.g. in this case the avoidance of punishment or disapproval. However, the later consequences of such an adjustment can be severe. For example our hypothetical child matures into an adult who has no curiosity about self or others; probably operates with strict rules of behaviour (e.g. 'Don't be nosey'; 'Leave well alone' etc.) that he or she expects others to comply with; probably feels resentful or angry when others show curiosity in him or her; and is likely to have a lot of difficulties when exposed to a learning event. The trainer encountering

such individuals could well believe that they are resistant to the programme or to learning generally, and having made no impression on
the person, could well believe that their training skills or expertise were
inadequate.

Each of us has made similar adaptations throughout our lives, maybe
not with such severe consequences as the example above. But each of
these adaptations is likely to affect our ability to learn and change. The
nature of these adaptations is nearer the surface, and hence available for
examination and review, when we are experiencing difficulties in learning, and more particularly, when we are actively resisting learning or
the prospect of personal change. These learning difficulties, or blocks, I
will look at in more detail later in the chapter. For the moment I want
to look at the types of interruptions to the cycle of need satisfaction.

There are five types of interruption—introjection, projection, confluence,
retroflection and deflection. Irrespective of type, interruptions are
momentary and normally unnoticed by the individual in whom they
occur. An observer's clue to interruptions is the myriad of physical
events that take place in the body and, above all, breathing interruptions
or irregularities. The reason for this can best be explained by offering
another view of the cycle of gestalt formation and destruction as illustrated in Figure 1.3.

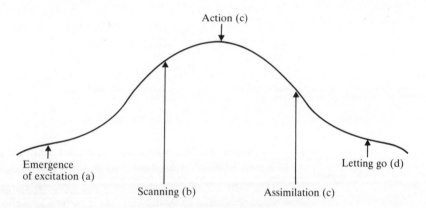

Figure 1.3 *The cycle of gestalt formation and destruction: another view*

As shown in Figure 1.3 as the need emerges (a) there is some physical
excitation (a dry throat for example), the person scans the environment
(b), takes action (c), satisfies the need (c), and then is ready to move on
to the next experience. Even if the cycle is interrupted (at any stage or
in any way) *the body will demonstrate both the excitation and the interruption
of the cycle.* A simple demonstration of this in action is what happens
when you decide not to show someone that you are angry. At such a
time you are likely to be talking through clenched teeth; you may be
making a fist (if necessary, behind your back); will be speaking in a
slow, deliberate voice; and will be tensing both your shoulders and
neck. Even if you are unaware of your anger many of these clues,
maybe in a subtler form, will be obvious to those around you.

Introjection   From birth we are confronted by a range of rules, standards, values and beliefs, about the ways in which we should, or should not, behave. Each one of these is a demand made upon us by the environment (parents, teachers, bosses etc.). Apart from rejecting or ignoring them there are two ways of dealing with these demands. The first response is assimilation—which involves selecting out of the mass those rules, or modifications, which can be accepted and absorbed as part of the self because they make sense, feel right, and are consistent with other values. The second response is introjection—which involves swallowing down rules and standards either because we are told to (and are punished and rewarded accordingly), or because they are fashionable or safe or revolutionary or traditional. These undigested attitudes, ways of acting, feeling and evaluating are called introjects.

Introjects give rise to two types of problems: first, they limit choices of behaviours with rules which are often irrelevant or impossible to attain. For instance, 'Be perfect' is a common introject in our culture. Second, it is possible to swallow potentially conflicting introjects ('Be nice to everyone' and 'Always tell the truth') which cannot be resolved at a theoretical or practical level. The result being intolerable tension.

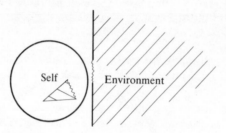

Figure 1.4   *Introjection*

These introjects involve, as Figure 1.4 demonstrates, giving up part of our self to accommodate part of the environment.

Like any other profession trainers have developed their own particular introjects. Some common ones are: 'Every course member should learn from a programme'; 'The trainer should be patient and accepting of every course member'; and 'The trainer should not show his or her feelings or responses to course members'. Every novice trainer quickly picks up these rules and standards and then discovers the impossibility of adhering to them. Many of these introjects are not clearly stated but are offered at an implicit level which makes them more difficult to deal with critically. At this level they make sense and are unlikely to be reviewed. When you hear someone say, 'It's a well-known fact that . . .', or 'That's the way the world is', then you are listening to the echo of an introject.

Projection   As introjection is the tendency to make the self a host for what actually is part of the environment, so projection is the tendency to make the environment a host for what originates in the self (see Figure 1.5). For example, as a 'good' trainer I always try to be patient with course mem-

bers (even if it is a burden) but one thing that I cannot
impatient course member who always wants me to hurry
activity, and I find it very difficult to know how to respon
with such individuals! The fact that I am unaware of my i
project that on to those around me does make such a pers
deal with.

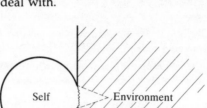

Figure 1.5 *Projection*

The projector's assumption about the other may well be founded on
some reality of observable behaviour. The impatient trainer is likely to
meet many impatient course members.

It is also possible for individuals to use this mechanism on themselves.
For projectors have a tendency not only to disown the impulse, but also
to disown that part of the self in which the impulse arises. In disowning
the part and giving it an objective existence outside the self they are
able to avoid taking responsibility for the problem. So, for instance,
trainers who complain after a session 'This group has given me a head-
ache', neatly sidesteps the responsibility of giving themselves a head-
ache by passing it on to that part of the self that does the talking!

Confluence

Confluence is a word taken from geology and describes a flowing
together, the merging of two rivers. In Gestalt, the word describes the
situation when the individual has no clear sense of boundary between
the self and the environment (see Figure 1.6). When confluent the
individual operates from a kind of emotional and perceptual colour-
blindness. Newborn infants live in confluence, they have no sense of
any distinction between inside and outside, between the self and other.
A common example of confluence is the person who absurdly identifies
himself with another person—protesting, in spite of all contradictory
evidence, that they are exactly alike. The contradictory evidence is
either ignored or dismissed by the individual. Some organizations
actively promote confluence by demanding a strong, but narrow, sense
of loyalty from their employees. A form of loyalty which requires
unthinking identification with the management view, and the avoidance
of all forms of conflict, breeds corporate confluence. The consequences
to the organization are loss of creativity and an inability to respond to a
changing business environment.

One of the recurring problems facing trainers at the start of any programme is the tendency of most groups to develop confluence, not only
with each other, but also with the trainer. The reason for this is the

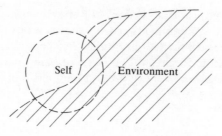

Figure 1.6 *Confluence*

natural desire for safety and security that each of us brings to joining a new group. This desire, if not properly managed by the trainer, can lead to either the group excluding the trainer because he or she is encouraging them to learn through paying attention to their differences and not their similarities, or the trainer may end up being seduced into being a host or hostess to the group rather than take the risk of being a trainer. A good indication of this kind of pressure is the resistance we can marshal when someone attempts to interrupt any pattern of our habitual behaviour, e.g. taking a particular route to work, or the way in which we carry out a routine task. Any habitual pattern of behaviour bears the hallmark of confluence and is unlikely to be surrendered easily or willingly.

To return to the three members of the interviewing panel, mentioned at the start of this chapter, each one of them was confluent with both their judgemental impulses and with each other. The attempts of myself and other group members to offer feedback was unsuccessful because the recipients could (would) not see the event in the same way. To give up confluence requires a willingness to step into the unknown and will only be taken if the discomfort level of the confluent behaviour exceeds the imagined level of behaving in a different way. Until that point is reached the negative consequences of the present (in this example, feedback) can be rejected, distorted, suppressed or minimized by the person.

Confluence, as an interruption, is always a characteristic of the other interruptions, and for this reason it is sometimes described as a secondary state rather than a separate type of interruption. Whatever the theoretical distinction, confluence is a major hurdle to learning and personal change.

Retroflection
To retroflect literally means 'to turn back sharply against'. When people retroflect behaviour they treat self as they originally wanted to treat other persons or objects. Instead of using energy to manipulate and bring about changes in the environment to satisfy needs the energy is turned inwards with the same, but unrealistic, purpose (see Figure 1.7). To feel angry with another and refuse to express it means that the anger is turned inward and becomes feelings of guilt, sadness, inadequacy etc. This process is often signalled by furrowed brows, muscular tension or stiffness and the frequent use of the word 'myself' (e.g. 'I am ashamed

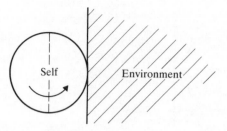

Figure 1.7 *Retroflection*

of myself', or, 'I have to force myself to do this job'). All statements of this sort are based on the surprising conception that I and myself are two different people. When people leave meetings and complain about being bored or criticizing the behaviour of other team members or the chairperson, they are likely to have spent much of their time at the meeting retroflecting.

It is not only 'bad' feelings which are retroflected but also 'good' feelings, like the giving and receiving of care, affection, and support. For example, people who are unable or reluctant to seek comfort from others will comfort themselves by stroking their own arm, leg or face. Because of some of the introjects in our culture (e.g. 'Be kind to others'; 'Big boys don't cry'; 'Women should be caring') each of us carries a classification scheme of both 'good' and 'bad' feelings as well as behaviour. One of the consequences of this is that when we experience a 'bad' feeling (e.g. anger, irritation, annoyance, contempt etc.) it is a small step to begin criticizing yourself for having the 'bad' feeling. This process of self-criticism—seemingly encouraged from birth—has a pernicious effect both on our image of ourself and on our level of confidence. Unfortunately, one of the effects of much of the current training in assertion skills (how to be assertive and influence others) actually feeds this process of self-denigration by encouraging people to think that assertion is 'good' and that being non-assertive or aggressive is, by extension, 'bad'. It would appear, from experience, that saying to people, 'It's OK to be non-assertive *or* assertive *or* aggressive' is both more helpful to them as people as it is more realistic to them as learners.

Deflection   Deflection involves the individual acting as if there was a screen between him or her and the rest of the world (see Figure 1.8) The role of the screen is to deflect any direct contact from other people. In that sense it both protects and keeps others at a distance. These deflections can take many forms:

- taking the heat out of a situation (e.g. 'There is no reason to be upset')
- being abstract or polite (e.g. 'Let's not be drawn into this debate')
- minimizing an emotion or a need (e.g. 'It's not important')
- talking about the possibility of having an emotion rather than acknowledging that you are experiencing it now

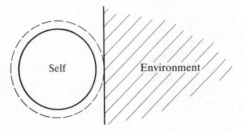

Figure 1.8 *Deflection*

- being diplomatic (e.g. 'I think we need to move on to another item')
- grandiosity (e.g. 'That just proves what a failure I am')
- denying emotions (e.g. 'We need to be rational and adult about this')

Again many of these behaviours are encouraged in our society, not least by our dubious heritage of the need for a stiff upper lip. Indeed, there are times when it is appropriate to use these and all the other interruptions. The problem arises, however, when we interrupt ourselves habitually and are not aware of what we are doing; for example, always being diplomatic and living with the consequences of, perhaps, stored resources of frustration, irritation, impatience, agitation etc., which, apart from the continual denial of the underlying needs, have a tendency to 'leak out' with the wrong people at the wrong time.

Although it is possible to distinguish between and to describe the five different types of interruption, it is important to say that they rarely occur in isolation. An individual is likely to compound the process of interrupting the cycle of need fulfilment, for example, with combinations of introjects ('I must not show my feelings'), retroflection (clenching the jaw to hold back anger), and deflection ('You may have a point there'). As already mentioned, whatever the combinations one feature of confluence is that it is always present as a secondary state to the other interruptions.[8]

Checklist for effective contact
1 Am I 'talking about' (e.g. theorizing or generalizing) instead of 'talking to' (e.g. asking for what I want, or, being personal)?
2 Am I lecturing the other person about what *ought* to be rather than dealing with *what is*?
3 Am I saying, 'I can't', when I really mean 'I won't'?
4 Am I asking a rhetorical question, pretending that I am looking for information, when I really want to make a statement?
5 Am I saying 'you, we, one, people, they' when I mean 'I'?
6 Am I talking about the past when the issue is in the present?
7 Am I saying where I stand on the issue?
8 Am I saying 'maybe' or 'possibly' when I really mean 'no'?
9 Do I stop when I have made my point, or do I elaborate with examples and reasons?
10 Am I 'broadcasting' into the air, or to a group in general, rather than talking directly to the person I am addressing?

11 Do I send mixed messages (e.g. express anger with a smile on my face)?

12 Am I really seeing and hearing what is happening now or am I thinking about the past or the future?

Learning blocks

The role of interruptions in the process of learning and personal change is vitally important, and for a number of reasons. (1), each of the behaviours which manifest an interruption are learnt behaviours and each one was learnt in response to a critical event in our lives (e.g. how to adjust to a powerful authority figure). (2), each of these behaviours stops us seeing the world as it really is now. Whatever the similarities, the boss–subordinate relationship has fundamental differences to the parent–child relationship. Not least, the subordinate has more resources and choice than the child. (3), at the time of the interruption we are unable to see the world clearly and cannot see the infinite range of choice available moment by moment. In this respect, we see what we want to see and miss what may be obvious to those around at the time. (4), each interruption demonstrates an implicit desire for the individual and his or her world to stay the same as he or she has experienced it over the years. Whatever the cost may be to me and others when I retroflect my desire for care at least I know from experience that I can survive as a result of behaving in this way. If I choose to behave in a different way, i.e. ask for care, I may be laughed at or rejected, and I may not be able to survive that possibility. Or if I have developed a view that effective managers are decisive, non-emotional, judgemental and ruthless, then simply to be presented with an alternative model of management by an enthusiastic trainer can be as critical as being told directly that my behaviour is inappropriate. At such times it makes a lot of sense that I choose not to learn.

This recognition that a failure to learn is often as active a process of choice as learning—this latter being a notion that all trainers subscribe to—offers different insights into managing a learning process. Indeed, I would go further and say that if trainers encouraged their groups to look at the many creative ways groups have *for not learning* then the effectiveness of any learning event would be significantly increased.

As an experiment you might like to reflect on a recent formal learning activity (training programme, lecture, book, counselling, etc.) that you experienced that proved to be a failure for you. At the time what kind of comments did you make to yourself:

• about the presenter (or author)?
• about the material?
• about the structure and presentation?
• about other factors (e.g. timing of the event, environmental conditions, relevance to work etc.)?

Having thought about your answers to the above questions you might become aware of a particular pattern in how you stop yourself learning.

Some common patterns are the following:

Block	*Examples*
Generalizing	Everyone has this problem; all this material is old hat.
Talking about	A friend of mine had a similar problem and she. . . .
Rigid expectations of self and others	I think I have a right to. . .; I must understand this fully.
Blocking awareness of self	Of course it does not worry me in slightest.
Blocking awareness of others	Jean looks perfectly happy to me (Jean is on the verge of tears).
Self-interrupting	Jumping from one point to another; agitation; withdrawal.
Catastrophizing	I couldn't possibly do that, she would never speak to me again.
Imagining unreal constraints	My boss would not let me do that.
Projecting	The trouble with you is that you are too damned aggressive.
Minimizing	It's not really important.
Archaic rules	I must never. . . .
Internal conflict	I should do this but I don't want to.
Theorizing	But how does this fit with the theory of X?
Denial	What problem?
Rejection	It could not possibly work.
Procrastination	On the one hand. . . on the other; I need to think.
Confusion	It seems so complicated.
Moralizing	This should not be allowed; I totally disagree with that.
Introjection	This is wonderful.

Thinking back on the situation what was the 'it' you chose not to learn, e.g. a need to be different, a need to break a habitual pattern, a need to give up some aspect of certainty or personal security, a need to feel superior or inferior?

In one of my early programmes as a 'professional' trainer at a management college I found myself stuck with a recalcitrant group who simply rejected everything offered and complained that the course was a waste of time and that they were not learning one new thing. Having battled with them for two days in a vain attempt to prove the worth of the course (and my worth as a trainer) I asked each member of the group to tell me how they stopped themselves learning. Their reasons, which were initially couched in terms of what I had failed to do, were variations of the list above. As I logged their answers on the flipchart a significant number of the group began to take responsibility for their contribution to the impasse. The intervention proved to be a turning point in the life of the group. What emerged from the discussion was their resentment at having been sent on the course and a desire to prove to themselves, and each other, that they were not in need of remedial training.

Conditions for learning and change

There is a requirement to establish some basic conditions to facilitate learning and personal change. The first set of conditions are to do with the individual—how he or she feels about self. The second set of conditions are to do with the environment—physical and emotional.

To return to the cycle of need fulfilment: each round of a particular cycle starts in response to an excitation or impulse which has a physical characteristic (for example, a dry throat in the case of thirst). For the psychological and emotional needs there is an interrelated physical and emotional component. For example, my need for comfort is likely to manifest itself through the emotion of sadness which in turn I will become aware of through, say, a sensation of emptiness in my diaphragm, slow and laboured breathing, a self-stroking of my arms or face, and tears at the corner of my eyes. The emotional and physical aspects of my need occur at the same time, i.e. I recognize my emotion of sadness by the physical signs. Even if I interrupt my need for comfort, at any stage of the cycle, both my emotion and the physical characteristics of my repression of that need will be present, even though I am not aware of them. My body will be demonstrating clues about the need and its repression.

At each stage of the cycle it will be *as if* I will be making a series of 'go' or 'no-go' decisions. So at the first stage (*New situation*) I may experience some quality of dissatisfaction or discomfort which I can either stifle or allow to emerge. At the next stage (*Need*) I can allow the figure to form or interrupt that process (by thinking or distracting myself). If I allow the figure into the next stage of *Awareness* (recognize that I want comfort, for instance) I can decide to go on or stop. I can make similar decisions at the stages of *Organized action* or *Contact and satisfaction*. What will affect my decisions at each stage will be the respective levels of my anxiety and excitement about going forward. Simply, if my level of anxiety exceeds that of my excitement then I will interrupt the process. To stay with the example of my need for comfort: if the prospect of asking another person for comfort is too fearful (e.g. I may be rejected, or be seen as weak by the other person) then I will block the need. If my level of excitement is higher then I will take the risk. It is important to recognize that both anxiety and excitement are usually present in the cycle of need fulfilment and their respective levels can change second by second. The degree of change will be affected by what the person sees, or chooses to see, in the environment around them.

The second, though interrelated, set of conditions affects our ability to learn and change. The key environmental issues, in this respect, are support and challenge. The former is necessary to manage anxiety, the latter is necessary to focus the excitement. If trainers do not offer appropriate and well-timed interventions of challenge and support then they are not providing the appropriate conditions for learning and personal change. It appears, from my experience, that this is the area where trainers experience the most difficulty in carrying out their role. They either over-support or over-challenge or have problems in knowing when to do either. One reason for this difficulty is that trainers, in my judgement, do not pay sufficient attention to the nature of their relationships with each learner. They will either offer the same kind of 'professional' relationship to each person—seeing 'professional' as comprising a relationship based on distance, impartiality, and the application of expertise. Or they will simply pay attention to the group as if the characteristics of the group were shared equally by all the members, i.e. a 'difficult' group contains ten 'difficult' course members.

Summary

This chapter has looked at the process of learning, and has suggested that the theories of learning used by most trainers do not adequately account for the practical difficulties that frequently emerge when working with individuals and groups. In seeking to overcome these difficulties I have described how an understanding of both Gestalt psychology and Gestalt therapy can contribute to a more effective management of learning events. Some of the major concepts are described and are illustrated by examples drawn from training experience. In particular, I have concentrated on the types of learning difficulties that we experience when attempting to change or develop new knowledge, skills, and attitudes. In exploring these problems I have explained that the trainer needs to establish a number of conditions to facilitate learning. The trainer's ability to create these conditions will be largely determined by the kind of relationship that is offered to the learner. Therefore, in the next chapter I want to look at the nature of the relationship between the trainer and learner.

References

1. David A. Kolb *et al.*, *Organisational Psychology: A Book of Readings* (Prentice-Hall, 1971).
2. Peter Honey and Alan Mumford *Manual of Learning Styles* (Peter Honey, 1982).
3. Edward W.L. Smith (ed.), *The Growing Edge of Gestalt Therapy* (Citadel Press, New Jersey, 1977).
4. Frederick S. Perls, *In and Out of the Garbage Pail* (Bantam Books, 1972).

5. Frederick S. Perls, *Ego, Hunger and Aggression* (Vintage Books, New York, 1969).
6. Frederick S. Perls, Ralph F. Hefferline and Paul Goodman, *Gestalt Therapy* (Pelican, 1973).
7. J. Wysing and E. Rosenfield (eds), *An Oral History of Gestalt Therapy* (*The Gestalt Journal*, Special issue, 1982).
8. Neil Cark and Tony Fraser, *The Gestalt Approach*, 2nd edn (Roffey Park Institute, 1987) (note: the figures and some of the examples of interruptions have been adapted from Chapter 4).

2 Trainer as change agent

Before looking in detail at the role of the trainer as change agent it is important to review the kind of relationship that the trainer has with the learner. The reason for such a review—and this will prove to be a central argument throughout the book—is that the relationship between the trainer and learner is the major determinant of the effectiveness of any learning and personal-change strategy. The ability to establish an appropriate relationship is more important than any skills or expertise the trainer may have in the areas of training, consultancy or counselling. This is not to imply that such skills or expertise are unnecessary or invalid but that they need to be used in the service of what I shall subsequently describe as a helping relationship.

The traditional relationship

The kind of relationship which the trainer tends to develop with the learner is one of instrumentality, i.e. an expert who does things to and for others. Some of the characteristics of this role are:

1 Defining the aims or objectives of the learning event; where the trainer is not responsible for definition he or she is likely to be pursuing the aims established by a significant authority figure in the organization.
2 Defining the learning methodology of the programme—the ways in which people will learn; defining the content and structure of the programme—even if the structure is one that encourages learners to specify their own needs and ways of learning.
3 Choosing activities and interventions which encourage individuals and groups to learn in the ways which have been established by the trainer.
4 Choosing interventions which, explicitly or implicitly, reward appropriate learning behaviours and punish inappropriate behaviours (such punishments may include: confronting, ignoring, discounting, or labelling of the individual as a deviant).
5 Essentially being guided by his or her own needs—to be in control, to be seen as expert, to be perceived as helpful or powerful or friendly etc.

In my experience the role that I have defined above pervades the majority of learning events, be they to do with the acquisition of skills, knowledge or attitudes. It is a familiar role, one that can be seen in a variety of professions (doctor–patient; social worker–client; architect–customer; computer analyst–line manager etc.). Central to all these professions is a relationship based on expert and non-expert. Built in to each of these relationships is an understanding that the client/patient/ customer will defer to the expertise of the professional.

Unfortunately, the particular expertise that the trainer has aggrandized (how to learn, how to manage people and organizations) is not one that the learner is ready and willing to concede in the way that a patient is likely to do with a doctor. Nor, to be fair, does the average trainer feel comfortable with the mantle of expert in the way that other professionals do with theirs. One of the reasons for this—dare I say, healthy reluctance—is that training is still far from being recognized as a profession. Despite the recent efforts of both the Institute of Personnel Management and the Institute of Training and Development, most of the current practitioners are people who have no qualifications and have drifted into the role from other professional or technical backgrounds. In many ways the trainer is still an amateur in a world of professionals.

The result is that the trainer attempts to carry out the instrumental role described above without any great conviction. The learner is also likely, and rightly, to challenge the trainer in this role. Because of this the trainer is less able to hide behind the role of expert, and in fact may even go out of his or her way to deny the existence of their expertise *while actually attempting to carry out the role.*

One clear demonstration of this ambiguity has been the adoption and advocacy of the role of the non-directive trainer. I have already referred to this in the Introduction (see p. xiii). The basis of this role is to find as many ways as possible to pass responsibility for learning over to the learner by encouraging him or her to identify both what the learning needs are and how to satisfy those needs. All interventions made by a non-directive trainer are likely to be variants of 'What do you think?', 'How would you approach the problem?', or 'What do you need to do?' In spite of the fact that this approach may appear to be sanctioned by some worthy humanistic principles—e.g. the need to learn to cope with uncertainty; each individual needs to recognize their own expertise; the individual is the only one to know the answer to his or her problem etc.—my major concern about this approach is that it represents a detachment by the trainer from the world of the learner. What develops is a relationship based on maintaining a distance. In its own way a relationship as instrumental as that of the expert and non-expert. But with the additional problems that, (1), the trainer denies his or her expertise and, (2), the trainer makes a virtue out of frustrating the needs of the learner.

To illustrate some of the paradoxes inherent in this traditional role I would like to describe a programme that I was involved with for a number of years at a management college. This programme, 'Interpersonal relationships in organizations', was one of the most effective courses run by the college. It was designed for a maximum of twelve managers and supervisors and its aims were:

1 To develop awareness of self.
2 To develop awareness of others.

As this programme has been described in detail elsewhere[1] I will confine myself to saying that it was an unstructured programme based on a mixture of T-group (i.e. attention was paid to group dynamics) and Gestalt (individuals volunteered for personal process work). At some stage in the five days a theory input on Transactional Analysis was also provided to assist the learning process. The framework of the programme was provided by Gestalt ground rules for learning. There was an elaborate screening process before delegates could attend but once they arrived it was very clear that they had to adopt the prescribed method of learning (i.e. experiential and non-directive). The role of the trainers was to both police and support delegates through what to most of them was a difficult and strange learning process. One of the paradoxes, for both trainers and delegates, was the conflict between a sincerely held belief in respecting individuality alongside the obvious coercion of all people to learn in the prescribed method. Although as trainers we respected the rights of individuals not to learn, both our professional pride plus the expectations of the college and the nominating organization that delegates *would* learn meant that we used many sophisticated, and more basic, interventions to coerce people into learning. Because of the emotionality of the learning process the group also put 'deviants' under pressure to abide by the rules. Some courageous individuals did truly exercise their 'right' and chose to leave the programme. In the light of later experiences I now have doubts about the value and effectiveness of the learning that took place on these programmes. While I am clear that a number of individuals did genuinely gain insights into themselves and others, and were able to make changes in themselves and their relationships, both the pressurized environment and the speed at which we worked leave me wondering about the ability of delegates to transfer their learning to the work situation.

A second paradox that became apparent in our work was the conflict between, on the one hand, a realization that personal learning is most effective when focused at the level of helping people understand the ways in which they *resist* learning; and on the other hand, the inexorable pressure to push people through their respective resistances in order for them to conform to the prescribed method of working. So, for example, the learner who dealt with relationships purely on a cognitive level would receive feedback about that pattern but would then be 'encouraged' to express his or her feelings to others in the group. Such a short-cut in the learning process was clearly to help us, the trainers, rather than the learner.

The difficulties and paradoxes of the traditional relationship between trainer and learner will continue to limit the effectiveness of the training and development services until the nature of that relationship is drastically changed. For too long trainers have avoided looking at that issue. Instead attention has centred on the technology used and the packaging of the message. All forms of training—from the pedagogic to the experiential—have been characterized by a search for the panacea. Old ideas are repackaged; new forms of training have been developed (e.g. interactive video), and techniques and ideas have been pillaged from many disciplines (including psychotherapy), in a vain search for the answer.

In my own field, interpersonal skills training, there has been a steady procession in the last fifteen years of failed panaceas. In chronological sequence these have included: T-groups, Encounter groups, Transactional Analysis, Behavioural Analysis, Gestalt, Neuro-Linguistic Programming, Behaviour Modification, and Eriksonian hypnotherapy. Each has been tried and found wanting. Such a casualty list might suggest that they represent possible answers to the wrong question.

The helping relationship

At first sight it may appear to be a mistake to look at the world of psychotherapy for a model of a more effective relationship between the trainer and the learner. Certainly, the original psychotherapy model of the Freudian analyst and patient is as instrumental as any other relationship between a professional and a client. And in some ways it is worse. The roles are clearly defined (expert and non-expert) and the relationship is built on keeping distance. Although this does remain as a model for much of psychotherapy, the nature of that relationship has been examined in some detail by a number of approaches and found to be wanting. One example of this has been the development of Co-counselling by Harvey Jackins[2] which, among other things, attempts to determine the relationship between counsellor and clients as one of equals. Learners work in pairs and offer to be counsellors and clients as required by their partner. This kind of relationship is also evident in the wide establishment of self-help groups in the 1970s and 1980s. This wider movement not only aims to empower people but also provides a salutary corrective to the dangerous hegemony of professionalism. Fundamental to all professions is the clear assumption that the first task of any professional is to define the nature of the relationship with the client. What this model of equality does not address clearly, however, is the reality of the expertise owned by the professional. On the one hand, as a learner, I am unlikely to feel dependent on or intimidated by a peer; but on the other, I would like to gain access to the expertise of a professional *provided it is offered in a way* that does not leave me feeling one down to him or her and having to submit to the kind of relationship that they will determine.

In recent years Gestalt therapists, most notably Gary Yontef and the Gestalt Therapy Institute of Los Angeles,[3] have sought to develop a model of relationship that does facilitate the learning process. Their model, the dialogic relationship, has been derived from the work of Martin Buber[4] on what he described as the 'I–Thou' relationship. I have worked with this model in the context of Gestalt therapy, both as therapist and patient. For me the hallmarks of this approach are trust, warmth, patience and respect. Because of my experiences I have consciously applied it in the contexts of training, counselling and consultancy. Although it is a model developed by therapists I believe that it provides guidelines for any relationship that is based on helping people to learn and change.

The characteristics of this relationship, as described by Yontef, are as follows.

Inclusion   Trainers respect the moment-by-moment experiences of learners (their
                  thoughts, feelings, perceptions, attitudes) and attempt to see the world
                  as through their eyes. To do this effectively means that trainers have to
                  put to one side (i.e. 'bracket') their own perspective on what is happen-
                  ing or being described. So if learners describe a training activity as irrel-
                  evant or useless it is important that trainers discover how the former
                  made that judgement. Or, to return to a learning problem described in
                  Chapter 1 (see pp. 2–3), if learners perceive that they are asking non-
                  judgemental questions, then trainers need to 'bracket' their own
                  judgements about that experience in order to understand how learners
                  discriminate between different kinds of questions. Despite the obvious
                  difficulties involved in seeing the world through the eyes of another—
                  not least when they are making judgements about you or what you
                  have done—the effort involved helps you to understand the person
                  (rather than what you believe to be true about them). The benefits for
                  learners are that they are truly listened to and offered the minimum of
                  respect. Such a response from the trainer helps them to feel more
                  secure and safe in a strange environment.

                  Inclusion has similarities to what Carl Rogers[5] has described as 'uncon-
                  ditional acceptance', i.e. accepting the other person for who they are and
                  not putting them under pressure to meet your expectations.

Presence   In addition, all the material that the trainer 'brackets' in conversation
                  and all his or her views, perceptions, ideas and expertise should be
                  offered as appropriate *in the service of the learner*. These contributions
                  should be offered as information that the learner can use, accept, dis-
                  card or modify as he or she thinks fit. If the learner accepts and uses
                  the information then the trainer is facilitating the learning process; if the
                  information is discarded or rejected the trainer is still facilitating the
                  learning process. Acceptance of this kind of 'rejection' is often difficult
                  for the trainer to handle, particularly if he or she believes that their own
                  level of self-worth is dependent upon being seen to be 'helpful'. But
                  working in this way does overcome the sterile debate of effective trainers
                  being either directive or non-directive when working with individuals
                  or groups. For the respective values of being directive or non-directive
                  will be determined by the learner and not the trainer. Most learners will
                  require both kinds of service from the trainer on different issues and at
                  different times.

                  The characteristic of presence deals with two of the problems apparent
                  in the traditional role of the trainer. First, it makes a virtue out of offer-
                  ing yourself as a person (being genuinely who you are) rather than as a
                  distant professional. Second, the encouragement to offer expertise in
                  this way—allowing the learner to assess the value—overcomes the
                  problem of denying or discounting the existence of any expertise. The
                  value for the learner of this approach is that he or she experiences
                  themself in a relationship with a person who, apart from being genuine,
                  offers a relationship based on equality in which the learner can exercise
                  as much choice as the trainer.

Commitment to dialogue

Within the framework of any programme or learning event the trainer does not attempt to control or shape the nature of the learning. The trainer may offer an activity, exercise, or theory input, but what is important about each and any of these structures is what the learner derives from the experience. Being willing to listen to what the learner is interested in at any time is an acquired skill. Some years ago I ran a listening-skills exercise for a group of trainers. In reviewing the experience which was judged by them to be unsuccessful, what I 'heard', in addition to their complaints, was that they were talking about their difficulties in listening. I therefore offered them an exercise based on their avoiding listening for a period of twenty minutes. Apart from the novelty of being asked not to listen, the group derived a great deal of benefit from the activity, because their attention was focused on the problems of listening, *not* on the skills of effective listening. For me it demonstrated the value of choosing to listen to what they wanted rather than expecting them to work in a way that I decided was appropriate.

It might appear contradictory that within the context of a structured training programme I am advocating that the learner's needs should take priority. This contradiction might even appear to be specious after the criticisms made earlier of the non-directive approach to training. But I do believe that there needs to be a point of balance between the two extremes of, on the one hand, the trainer-centred approach (the trainer determining what should be learned and how) and, on the other hand, the learner-centred approach (the learner determining what should be learned and how). What characterizes both extremes is the lack of dialogue between the learner and the trainer. The trainer, clearly owning his or her expertise, can offer in that dialogue structure, safety, support and guidance. While the learner offers a willingness to explore his or her needs and feels comfortable to accept, modify or reject what the trainer has to offer. The nature and course of that dialogue is then shaped by the interaction between them with neither exercising control on the learning or each other.

One of the clearest areas on any training programme where this kind of interaction can be closely monitored is where time is allocated for workshop activities. The workshop element is something I have been experimenting with for the last seven years. (For a detailed example of this approach see p. 54 for a description of the 'Personal Development Programme' for the Milk Marketing Board.) At the start of the workshop participants are asked to express their preferences for (1) what specific skill or behaviour they want to explore or develop; (2) what learning approach they would like to adopt (role play, skills exercise, personal awareness work by exploring their relationships with other members of the group, brainstorm session, feedback from other group members etc.); and (3) whom they would like to involve from the group in their learning activity. The workshop is offered after a minimum of twenty-four hours of a programme which should ensure that the participants are likely to have a fairly clear idea of what they want, and feel safe enough in the group to exercise responsibility for their learning. As a trainer running such workshops I essentially take a responsive role, i.e. helping individuals to clarify their wants, offering structures and ideas, managing time and the feedback activities. The key training skill required to run these kinds of workshops is that of truly listening to each participant, not only in terms of what they are actually saying, but also to what they are having difficulty saying. For example, a recent participant on an influencing skills programme started to identify her learning need as:

I want to learn how to cope with authority figures. I usually feel one-down and intimidated when I have to talk to one of the *big* bosses. (My emphasis)

What I paid particular attention to in her statement was the word 'big', and I asked her to expand on this. What she subsequently said was that she actually felt scared when in the presence of tall, severe looking men, *irrespective* of their organizational role and position in the hierarchy. Whenever she encountered such people she invested them with an authority that she denied herself. This clarification opened up a number of learning possibilities—all the men in the group, including me, were taller than she, and our perceived degree of severity was an area to explore. She acted upon my suggestion to offer all the men feedback on how she perceived us and how she felt in response to each of us.

By choosing to listen to what she found difficult to say there were two obvious benefits. First, we avoided organizing a role play focused on the surface need of dealing with authority, which might or might not have picked up the more important issue about her fear of physical aggression from men. Second, once the need was clarified the choice of an appropriate learning activity was both obvious and simple. Throughout that conversation and the activity I felt as if I were involved in a shared and creative learning experience.

Non-exploitation

There are a number of ways (both subtle and gross) in which the trainer can exploit the learner, and of these, I want to examine four major areas; using the learner as a means to an end; using language to exclude; the trainer working beyond his or her limits of competence; and the trainer pushing the learner beyond their limits of comfort.

Using the learner as a means to an end

Exploitation starts as soon as the trainer begins treating the learner as an object—to be analysed, categorized, saved, transformed, manipulated, or as an example to encourage the others. This danger is particularly evident on interpersonal skills courses where the use of models and theories of behaviour implicitly, if not explicitly, encourages participants to label themselves and each other. Some models (e.g. Transactional Analysis,[6] Belbin's team roles[7]) are more pernicious than others in this respect, whatever warnings the trainer may offer participants about this danger. Even when such models are not introduced it is always seductive for any trainer to label individuals mentally as types or categories and then respond to them on that basis rather than choosing to see their individuality. In a previous book[8] I, and my co-authors, introduced the concept of the 'problem course member' and offered strategies for dealing with particular types. In retrospect, I recognize that the mere act of transferring *my* difficulty in coping with particular behaviours cannot be dealt with by labelling, not just the behaviour but the whole person, as a difficult course member. In a training situation (or any situation, for that matter) while the other person is responsible for his or her behaviour my ability to respond to them is my responsibility not theirs.

Similarly, choosing to view someone in need of help (whether they want it or not); using someone to demonstrate your skills or expertise; using someone as a vehicle for raising the risk level, or to move the group along in its development; are all manipulations, made worse and not better, by the faint odour of assumed altruism.

Underpinning much of this kind of exploitation is the self-deception of the trainer. Often the basis of this self-deception is a lack of clarity about the needs he or she is attempting to satisfy through choosing to help other people learn and change. For each trainer brings to that role a personal agenda—for power, influence, affection, respect, avoidance of learning and changing of self etc.—which contaminates both judgement and behaviour. The problem in each case is not the agenda item but his or her lack of awareness about the existence of the need.

Use of language Training, like any other profession, has a highly developed language drawn from a number of sources (organization theory, organizational psychology, management theory, therapies of many types etc.). Part of any programme is likely to involve offering some of this language to participants. But language, like any other form of information, is also a source of power. In the training situation this power can be misused in many ways—not least by imposing our language on the more important words of the learner, e.g.

Participant: People are motivated by a sense of achievement.
Trainer: You mean self-actualization.

It can also be misused in the following ways: by using language and not defining terms; by choosing not to explain what concepts or interpretations you are acting upon in any learning event which means that the learner is excluded from an important part of the learning process; and by choosing to see your language or concepts as being more important than the person or his or her language and experience. This problem is often apparent when the trainer offers feedback to the participant, e.g.

Trainer: I believe you are very task-centred with a directive management style.
Participant: Well, I am paid to do my work!

Apart from the language being exploitative, in this example, it also leads to a dialogue between the deaf.

Trainer working beyond his or her limits Trainers exploit learners by not paying attention to their own limitations. The first such limitation involves working beyond their current level of competence and expertise. One notorious area for this to occur is that of personal-skills training (e.g. influencing, counselling, facilitating) where the trainer can invite people into activities and experiences of emotionality on the simple assumption that catharsis is a learning experience, and not having the competence or expertise to be able to discriminate that whereas this may be true for some individuals, at some times, in some places, it can also be a questionable experience for many, and lead to long-term trauma for others. Similarly, dangerous generalizations are often made about people's ability to cope with intensive structured learning experiences which always involve some level of performance anxiety for individuals. I do not mean these comments to suggest that trainers should never push out their boundaries of risk—in fact we would deny our own learning if that prohibition stood—but there is a world of difference between trying something new (an exercise or intervention, say) and being irresponsible.

There are also times when the trainer is tired, unclear or simply confused. At such times there is often a temptation to be too demanding on individuals or groups, or, conversely, to look for short cuts or easy options. Under these circumstances, there are better ways of taking care of yourself and the group—for example, calling a break to a session or a day; asking your co-trainer to take the lead; lowering the risk level of sessions; offering a relaxation or fun activity; giving the group time to reflect on their learning or experiences so far on the programme; sharing your concerns with the group; asking the group to design and/or manage the session.

Pushing the learner beyond his or her limits

This form of exploitation often goes hand in hand with the one above. For a number of years there was a fashionable belief in training (unfortunately, it has not disappeared) that learning takes place when people are pushed to, or beyond, their limits. At one level, this was often acted upon as a result of an organizational imperative, the basis of this imperative being that if an organization is going to invest money in training, particularly residential programmes, then participants would be expected to work a sixteen-hour day. These marathons would often mean that participants could still be working till after midnight to prepare for the next day. I often suspect that the current vogue for outward-bound courses is partly based on this belief.

At another level, trainers heavily influenced by their experiences of some therapies or *their* understanding of them believe that learning and change can only take place if people are pushed through their resistances. As this is an area I want to look at in more detail later in this chapter I will simply confine myself to saying here that acting on such a belief means that the relationship between trainer and learner is one of exploitation.

There are also some more immediate practical concerns about the possibility of abusing the learner in a helping relationship. Not least is the ethical constraint of developing a sexual relationship. Like any professional relationship there is a position of trust and responsibility invested in the trainer, and, however effectively the trainer safeguards against the possibility of dependency, sexual invitations are likely to be offered. The paradox is often that the more effective you are as a trainer the more likely you are to receive such invitations. Similarly, the danger of attracting non-sexual groupies also needs to be guarded against. The helping relationship, as defined above, is often the most intimate kind of relationship that many people have experienced. But the intimacy, however, is purposeful (to aid learning), and despite its similarities to friendship and love it is of a different kind and involves different responsibilities.

Living the relationship

An essential characteristic of the helping relationship is the belief that each moment of contact between the trainer and the learner must be approached as a new experience. Whatever occurred in previous encounters—in the training room or outside—is merely a backcloth to the present. How I, as a trainer, am feeling now and experiencing the world now is different from my earlier experiences. How the learner is feeling now, and experiencing the world now, is different from his or her earlier experiences. Whenever we make contact all kinds of outcomes are possible. So if we were involved in an unproductive encounter before then this time may be more productive or less. If we meet at the right time and in the right way then we will both learn.

The importance of this characteristic is that it provides a necessary antidote against the self-fulfilling prophecy (i.e. if I believe that a task or a person will be difficult then it is likely to be so). It also provides a safeguard against the trainer using well-worn interventions or training activities that may have been effective elsewhere but which are no longer appropriate for this time, this person, or this group. The belief that a group of individuals have identical learning needs, even in such a restricted area like assertion, is a questionable assumption. The trainer who acts upon such a belief does a major disservice to learners. Therefore, personal-skills programmes based on offering a series of techniques or skills which are to be mimicked and practised until perfected tend to have the limited shelf-life of most perishable goods. What is missed in the learning process is the richness of individuality.

Any trainer who subscribes to this model of the helping relationship commits himself or herself to the task of developing a diversity of relationships with every group. Some of those relationships may be intimate, enjoyable, and mutually rewarding; some may be distant and purely functional; some may be of a brief intellectual encounter; some will involve difficulty and uncertainty; and some maybe like ships that pass in the night. The reason for this diversity will be the fact that whatever kind of relationship trainers offer, learners will also be choosing what they want from them. Whatever learners' needs are, in this respect, the least that trainers can do is to honour and value those needs. For many trainers this view is likely to confront and contradict what they believe to be a professional relationship based on impartiality and distance (i.e. attempting to be the same to everyone, in spite of the fact that they do have different responses to individuals). In some cases the need to hold on to this kind of professionalism is a defence against self-exposure, uncertainty, or taking risks. Even where that is not true then the trainer, in my view, unnecessarily limits the options for learning and change.

Checklist of the helping relationship
1 *Inclusion*
   Respecting the moment-by-moment experiences of the learner (thoughts, feelings, perceptions, attitudes) and be willing to see the world through their eyes. Putting on one side ('bracketing') our own experiences.
2 *Presence*
   Offering our own responses to the learner as appropriate, and *in the service of his or her needs.*

3 *Commitment to dialogue*
Allowing the pathway of the conversation to be determined equally
by both parties.
4 *Non-exploitation*
To avoid exploiting, manipulating, or leading the learner.
5 *Living the relationship*
Allowing the present to be a new beginning. Letting go of the past,
not shaping the future.

The change agent

Having offered the model of the helping relationship I would now like
to consider the purpose to which it addresses itself, i.e. the changing of
ideas, behaviour and attitudes. In particular, I wish to look at the process of resistance.

Although it is clear that the primary objective of any trainer is to
develop learning as a prerequisite for change, his or her role in that
process is less clear. In the different contexts (training, counselling and
therapy) the word 'catalyst' is often used as a synonym for the term
'change agent'. It is instructive to start with a dictionary definition of the
word:

catalyst: a substance which exerts a force on another substance thereby affecting
change on the latter without being changed itself.

This definition fits comfortably with what I have earlier defined as the
traditional role of the trainer but is at odds with that described in the
helping relationship. It implies that a person with truly remarkable powers
can enter into a social situation (a relationship, a training group, an
organization) and affect change through some form of influence and yet
remain impervious to being influenced. My own belief is that the trainer
or consultant who operates in this way may indeed affect change but:

1 the nature of the change strategy is being imposed on the client or
the client system;
2 if the trainer is impervious to influence or change then he or she is
not learning;
3 learning, if it does take place, is an incidental consequence of the
change strategy for the client or the client system;
4 there is no recognition that effective change is dependent on a learning strategy;
5 the client, or the client system, will inevitably reject the change
strategy—openly or covertly.

Most internal trainers are likely to have experienced situations where
the organization has called in an external consultant or agency to imple-
ment a change strategy which, like a transplanted organ, has been
rejected by the host body. The typical organizational response to such
failures is to subsequently find fault with the consultant, the package, or
the commitment of managers. Such failures spur them on to find a 'better'
consultant or a 'better' package. In this way they mirror those trainers
who get locked into the endless search for a panacea (see p. 22). It
seems that no matter how many times the cycle is repeated, those who

make the decisions do not seem to learn from the experience. This failure to learn, coincidentally, mirrors some of the organizational problems that the panaceas are expected to cure.

For this reason, if nothing else, I would suggest that one component of the change-agent role is to be a learner, and the first step in the learning process is to discover how this person, this group, this department, this organization, manages itself at the moment. How does he/she/it learn and change; and how does he/she/it resist learning and change? Not least the change agent needs to pay attention to how the client or client system affects and influences him or her. If I am asked to run an influencing skills programme for an organization then an important source of information for helping me to design and run such a programme is my experience of how the client and the client system influences me. For example, one client organization that I have worked for, albeit episodically over the years, could be described as having a culture appropriate to a 'gentlemen's club'. Members of this organization, by and large, are socially skilled, very polite, have a distaste of conflict and aggression, disguise ruthlessness with charm and notions of expediency, and tend to control through manipulation. Paying attention to how they influenced me, and my responses to that form of influence, provided me with grave doubts about offering them the kind of influencing skills programme that I currently provide for the Milk Marketing Board (see pp. 22–23).

A second component of the role of change agent is that of interaction, i.e. the change agent should be as open to change as the client or client system. My first project as an internal organization development consultant took place in a social services department of a local authority. My task was to help the department develop a more effective communications system, and my client was the director and his management team. In the course of the project—which lasted a year—I emerged with:

1 a detailed understanding of the role and problems facing social workers;
2 a deeply enriched view of counselling and group dynamics;
3 an awareness of how jargon and language can be used to exploit people;
4 an awareness of how the values of openness and honesty can be distorted to manipulate and punish people (e.g.

> *Case-worker*: I'm deeply worried about Mrs X and her children being evicted at 4.00 p.m. today.
> *Team leader*: Let's put Mrs X on one side for the moment. I'm concerned that you are using clients to meet your own needs. Let's talk about your problem. . .).

The third component of the role of change agent is to act as both reflecting mirror—this is what I see and notice; and as a licensed idiot—questioning the obvious (e.g. 'How does that work?', 'Why do you do that?'). But it is important to reflect back and question from a position of involvement and not of detachment and judgement.

Resistance to change

Any resistance to change or learning is typically seen by many trainers as totally negative behaviour and as something to be confronted, subverted, or managed in some way. In effect, the trainer decides to meet resistance with resistance—and, as such, mirrors the offending process. Such a view does not do justice to either the person resisting or demonstrate any understanding of the function of resistance or the nature of learning.

It is interesting to reflect that while most people will subscribe to the inherent value of any learning and will readily support the need for change, they are just as likely to accept their right to resist both. Many trainers at the start of a learning event take resistance to learning to be inevitable—something to be regretted and coped with.

Resistance, in psychotherapy, has been defined as: processes designed to protect the person from injury. It, therefore, serves the same function as that of checking tyre pressures on a car before starting on a journey, or of placing a guard before an open fire. The fact that the danger in learning is less apparent than either a car crash or setting the house on fire does not diminish the reality of the danger that we all can, and do, fear at such times. The risk of ridicule, censure, embarrassment, disapproval or loss of face is no less real than the prospect of tissue damage.

The fact that X believes himself to be at risk now (from a new idea, a piece of feedback, from having to perform in some way) is a reality. That others around him at the time do not experience the situation in the same way is of interest but does not invalidate X's fear. His fear needs respect and acknowledgement, not denial or dismissal. That he may choose to 'mask' his fear with anger, cynicism, hostility, avoidance or passivity often makes it difficult for those around—not least the trainer who sees him as a professional challenge—to be supportive or understanding.

To learn and change requires some measure of willingness, trust and support in ourselves and in those around us. For example, the manager who has doubts about her management style needs all these characteristics simply to make public her concerns. If, however, she is not willing even to raise her concern then all the feedback, ideas and suggestions in the world are likely to be wasted because at this time they are irrelevant. What is relevant now is how she chooses to resist, and what is the feeling that underpins the resistance—fear, anxiety, envy, guilt etc. At such a time the trainer would do well to offer support and guidance to help her understand, when she is willing, the nature of her resistance. The appropriate choice of management style is less important.

Some common processes of resistance have been recently described by Hunter Beaumont[9] in a lecture. These are:

Anxiety

Anxiety is a fear reaction caused by a belief that the present or near future is threatening. In animals fear is a responsive action to actual danger, whereas people have a much greater ability to anticipate the possibility of danger. Anxiety can be functional, e.g. looking both ways before crossing the road. It can also be dysfunctional:

- when the fear of what could happen does not reflect the possibility of the situation;
- when the person does not believe that he or she could cope with the situation;
- when there is a possibility of breaking an unquestioned rule about behaviour, e.g. trainers must be impartial;
- having a confused perception about what is happening.

Guilt   Guilt is an emotional reaction based on a sense of responsibility for someone else's suffering. Healthy guilt leads to remedial action, e.g. choosing not to tell lies. It can also be dysfunctional:

- when a sense of responsibility is based on a rule rather than a genuine response, e.g. I must finish this report;
- not taking remedial action, e.g. I keep telling him off and I must not do so;
- always putting the needs of others before your own.

Shame   Shame is an emotional reaction based on a belief that 'I have no right to exist'. Because of the intensity of this feeling people will go to extraordinary lengths to avoid the process, e.g. self-righteousness, blame, denial.

Envy   Envy is most easily observed among children but as we grow older we become more skilled at disguising the feeling, not just from others but from ourselves. In groups it can take many forms—sadness, anger, hurt etc., and is often a hidden agenda which has a profound effect on the development of the group.

Each one of these processes of resistance can be triggered off by the 'threat' of a new idea, attitude or skill. When resistance is most intense the person can experience a state of impasse—when he or she cannot make sense of what is happening both inside and outside themself at that moment. At such times all the senses may be disturbed and the dominant feeling is likely to be fear and a desire to escape. It is too easy to assume that such extreme conditions can only arise on unstructured personal-awareness programmes. I remember giving a theory presentation on the Gestalt interruptions described in the last chapter. At the end of the hour's session one course member sought me out. Obviously distressed and disorientated he said, 'I feel as if I have been mentally raped'. I then spent the best part of an evening helping him through the impasse.

I mentioned earlier in this chapter that there has been a vogue of trainers believing that learning only takes place when people are pushed through their resistances. My own positon is that not only is this unnecessary for learning purposes, it is also exploitative and potentially damaging. More effective choices for managing resistance are as follows:

1 Accept the need and right of the person to resist.
2 Make that acceptance explicit.
3 Encourage the person to learn about the process.
4 Help the individual to develop self-support, e.g. through effective breathing.

5 Offer appropriate support, e.g. time-out from the session, one-to-one conversation.

6 Develop more support within the group.

7 Encourage the person to test reality, e.g. 'What is the worst thing that could happen to you?'

8 Give the person time and freedom.

9 Tell him or her that you are concerned about them.

10 Listen carefully to what they say and believe every word.

11 Maintain contact at whatever level they feel comfortable with.

12 Accept the person and their right to resist you and your programme.

13 Encourage and support them if they wish to leave. This will mean providing support to them with their nominating or line manager.

People at risk

Without wishing to open a debate that I am unqualified to conduct (i.e. the nature of mental illness, categories of illness), I wish to look at a problem that concerns every trainer—people who are particularly vulnerable to learning events, and those whose behaviour make the prospect of learning too unsafe for others. It is too easy to make the assumption that employees of organizations, because they are able to pursue a career, have the basic coping mechanisms for dealing with learning and change. My own experience leads me to hold a contrary assumption, which is that many organizations find ways to collude with individuals to avoid the reality that they are suffering from an inability to cope with day-to-day pressures. Some typical organizational responses to such individuals are: structural isolation (through promotions or sideways moves); labelling individuals as 'difficult' or 'unsocial'; engaging them with unimportant tasks; or, offering them as challenges for newly promoted supervisors or managers. An equally likely response is to send them on programmes to be 'cured'. Such a prescription may be implicit or explicit. Not surprisingly, the individual concerned (whatever the problem) finds it difficult to cope. Often, under these circumstances the 'real' problem can be the nominating manager's and not the delegates.

It is possible to identify some particular categories of people who may be at risk. But I wish to avoid suggesting, in any way, that the situations or behaviours described below *automatically* mean that such individuals are always at risk. I have enough experience of individuals who have fitted these categories to know that they have approached a learning event with a positive view to change their behaviours and self-image.

There are five categories.

Vulnerability

Because of recent or current life experiences (e.g. bereavement, the ending of an important relationship, illness in a family, divorce or separation etc.) the individual is feeling emotionally raw and may well be marshalling their resistances as a way of taking care of themselves. Consequently, any pressures on them or any degress of emotionality by others in the group may have the effect of their feeling totally overwhelmed. An unprovoked catharsis (of tears, anger, despair etc.) could be followed by a profound sense of shame or guilt. The particular diffi-culty here is that the person concerned is least likely to talk about these events to the trainer or others in the group. Even when the person feels comfortable within himself or herself and wants to use the event as part of the healing process then other factors need to be considered, e.g. Does the contract for the programme include the opportunity for such disclosure? Is the group strong enough to support such learning? Is the trainer competent to handle such issues?

Total resistance   Most of us have times when we resist learning and change, but there are some individuals for whom resistance seems to be a life-or-death issue. It would appear, from the outside at least, that if the individual were to concede one learning point then the whole fabric of their inner world would be torn into shreds. Therefore, they resist, compulsively, and usually with great anger or scorn. Not only do they resist for them-selves but they do so on behalf of others. Typical behaviours may include questioning the value of theory or learning activities; denying or questioning the learning benefits of others (even when the learner is describing what he or she has learnt); and, describing as an unbridgeable chasm the difference between what happens now and the 'real' world outside. A common view they have of the world is that behaviour and consequences are fixed, therefore change is not possible. They are apt to use animal or military metaphors when describing behaviour, e.g. Life is a jungle or a battleground. Beneath the anger or hostility is likely to be a potentially overwhelming fear.

Psychiatric history   Again, like those who fall into the category of vulnerability, people with
or medication   a psychiatric history are unlikely to make that knowledge public. Those who do are the most likely to cope positively with the learning event. The people who need regular medication for stress or severe conditions usually, in my experience, make it known because the constraints of the timetable interfere with their pattern of treatment. The ideal situation for any trainer is for such individuals to tell them before the event so that the pair of them can talk through the problem and make an informed judgement about the appropriateness of attendance.

Behavioural   There is obviously a grey area for most of us between acceptable eccen-
problems   tricity and behaviour which disturbs others. Some of the behaviours that I have experienced which fall into the latter are: a degree of abstraction and theorizing which is impossible to follow; absent-mindedness which is both intense and prolonged; volcanic outbursts of happiness and/or depression; descriptions of experiences shared by the group which bor-der on the surreal; total and unchanging suspicion of everyone's motives; intense panic or chronic agitation; and a wide range of 'theatrical' behaviours (e.g. someone on all fours and barking like a dog). Whatever these behaviours reveal or conceal about the individual the immediate consequence is that they make a group, including the trainer, feel unsafe and thus resistant to learning. My own view is that unless the trainer can successfully contain the individual he or she should be asked to leave the programme. Such an intervention is in everyone's

interest, and any trainer who encourages such a person to explore the meaning of such behaviour is being foolish and irresponsible.

Persecutor Similarly, the person who compulsively punishes others (with ridicule, scorn or point-scoring) overtly or implicitly, has the same kind of threatening effect on the group. Often this kind of person is highly manipulative and can successfully set up conflicts between others. Because he or she can be manipulative they tend to operate outside the learning environment and away from the trainer. For this reason they can be difficult to spot. If a group appears to be unnaturally cautious or full of conflict then there is a chance that it contains a skilled persecutor. One of the consequences of such a person in a group is that he or she can offer a more powerful role-model than that of the trainer. In essence, it means that the pair of you compete for influence in the group. The best option for dealing with such a person is to raise the conflict or the competition within the group by confronting the individual about his or her behaviour. Avoidance of conflict, or, manipulation by the trainer, can create an unresolvable situation with the group being split or fragmented. With people like this I reserve the right to ask them to leave.

Whether these categories make sense to the reader or not—and I have concerns about categorising people—there are some behaviours, verbal and non-verbal, which are worth paying attention to:

- bizarre patterns of eye contact (relentless staring or complete failure to make eye contact);
- intense physical agitation (e.g. pacing or stalking around the room; tapping toes or hands);
- heavy tension in the musculature (particularly fists, arms and shoulders);
- compulsive confusion or statements about inability to understand what is happening or being said;
- gouging, pinching or punching of own body;
- insomnia;
- always isolating self from the group;
- failure to eat;
- or, drinking too much alcohol.

Clearly, many of us are likely to display some of these behaviours at different times but when they are compulsive or intense the chances are we cannot cope with what is happening. When the trainer picks up these signals it is always advisable to talk to the person alone, and well away from the group. If the person is finding it difficult to cope then it is worth suggesting that he or she go back to work, and for the trainer to be prepared, on their behalf or with them, to talk to the nominating manager about the decision to leave. (Often, knowing that he or she can be helped to leave will relieve the pressure that they are experiencing, and that knowledge helps them make a good decision to stay.) They may choose to stay on the clear understanding that, jointly with the trainer, they will monitor the situation. Finally, the trainer has the option to ask them to leave, if not in their interest but in those of the group. I know that many trainers will not exercise that choice (because they find it difficult to reject people, or, through professional pride, or because of the possible negative reactions to them by the group or the organization). My own experience of making that decision is that the majority of groups, irrespective of their initial reaction, will accept it if it is a good decision. Similarly, most nominators will accept on the same basis. The person who is asked to leave the event may have to deal with some negative consequences.

Summary

In this chapter I have defined the nature of the traditional relationship between the trainer and the learner as one of instrumentality, i.e. doing things *to* people. Having described some of the reasons for this approach, and how limiting it is for both parties, I have then described an alternative. This latter, which I have defined as a 'helping relationship', is derived from Gestalt therapy. The essential character of the helping relationship is that of working *with* the learner to manage jointly the process of learning and change. Having identified the five important characteristics of this relationship I have used this understanding to examine the nature of resistance to change. Finally, I have also discussed some categories of learner that are likely to present the trainer with particular problems.

In the next three chapters I will apply the helping relationships to the respective areas of training, counselling, and consultancy.

References

1. Neil Clark, Keri Phillips and Dave Barker, *Unfinished Business: The Theory and Practice of Personal Process Work* (Gower Press, 1984), Ch. 4.
2. Brigid Proctor, *Counselling Shop* (Burnett Books, 1978), chapter on Co-counselling.
3. G.M. Yontef, 'Gestalt Therapy: Its Inheritance from Gestalt Psychology' *Gestalt Theory*, Vol. 4, No. 1/2 (1982), 23–9.
4. Martin Buber, *I and Thou* (Charles Schribner's Sons, New York, 1970).
5. Carl Rogers, *On Becoming a Person* (Houghton Mifflin, Boston, 1961).
6. Eric Berne, *What do You Say after You Say 'Hello'?* (Corgi, 1975).
7. R.M. Belbin, *Management Teams: Why They Succeed or Fail* (Heinemann, 1981).
8. Clark *et al.*, *Unfinished Business*.
9. Hunter Beaumont, *Resistance as a Process*, Lecture given at Gestalt Therapy Institute of Los Angeles Summer Residential (21 July 1987).

3 The training relationship

For the trainer working in an organization the training relationship is one that includes three parties: the trainer, the learner, and the organization. Each one of these parties has a significant influence on the quality and effectiveness of each learning event that is provided. But only one of these parties—the trainer—can have a clear view of the nature of that relationship. Only he or she can know how the organization (specifically, those decision-makers in the organization who request, suggest, instruct the trainer to provide a service) inhibits or encourages the learning process. The simplest measure of this contribution can be read in looking at how delegates arrive on programmes. In broad terms, where delegates attend programmes—on the basis of having been involved in making a decision whether to attend or not; having been briefed on both the nature of the programme and the nominator's clear expectations of the learning benefits; seeing the learning event as being developmental rather than remedial; and, not feeling under pressure to be different as a result of the event—then the organization is making a vital contribution to that relationship. Where the above is absent, or worse, delegates arrive with the opposite experiences or expectations, then the basis of a healthy training relationship is severely compromised.

Trainers who are prepared to accept this kind of culture are not taking care of themselves or potential learners. Being prepared to invest time in developing the helping relationship with significant decision-makers is worth more in the long-term than adopting the strategy used by many trainers who seek to 'please' by running programmes at the first positive response by one of these people. Once the trainer gets locked into 'pleasing' authority figures in this way it becomes increasingly difficult to break the pattern of subservience. In my first post as an internal trainer I was soon put under pressure to justify myself by providing a range of courses (induction, interviewing skills, problem-solving, effective team working etc.). It would have been too easy to give in to these pressures and to have earned the approval of these decision-makers. But I was also aware that these prescriptions disguised two problems. First, I had no information about the needs of the learners. Second, the decision-makers were exempting themselves from the need to learn. My response was to spend time—about six months—to collect information from as many sources as possible and to establish a relationship with the decision-makers based on equality rather than my subservience. This simply involved talking with them about their view of the organization and their role and responsibility in the change process.

All organizations that I have worked in, or for, tend to have one of the following orientations to training:

Developmental—where learning and change is seen as a natural and continuing process which involves everyone in the organization.

Remedial—where learning and change is targeted on those unfortunates who cannot cope with present job demands.

Task-led—where learning and change is viewed as a simple process of consumption in which effectiveness is determined by the speed with which great numbers can be fed the latest message or idea.

Abdication—where learning and change is seen as the responsibility of one or more people, and is peripheral to the real tasks of the organization.

Each one of these approaches has a significant effect on *what* is provided and *how* it is provided. The trainer who sees learning and change as some kind of activity which is restricted to the training room is likely to spend a lot of time in that venue, and what he or she provides is likely to have a short shelf-life in the organization. The trainer, on the other hand, who is willing to manage the relationship with the organization (which is the briefest and best description of consultancy I know) is the one who is most able to create learning and change in the training room.

Having looked at the training relationship with the organization I now wish to concentrate on the helper–learner relationship in the context of a training programme. In particular, I want to look at how the helping relationship, as defined in the previous chapter, can be acted upon in all of the stages that a programme needs to go through.

Setting aims

The first issue about setting the aims has already been touched on in this chapter. And that is: who sets the aims? Ideally, it should involve three parties, with the trainer having special responsibility to turn the aims into actionable steps—something which can be measured, observed or experienced. There has long been a debate in skills and attitude training, particularly, about the inadequacies or irrelevance of attempting output measures on that kind of training. My own view is that any kind of training can and should be evaluated. For example, on many of the programmes that I offer, one of the learning aims is to develop self-confidence. Despite the fact that such an attribute cannot be quantified an increase of self-confidence can be both experienced and observed. My belief was put to the test when I was asked to design a junior management assessment centre which sought to measure, among other factors, confidence. The following is reproduced from the guidance notes for assessors:

Confidence—an ability to maintain self-belief when faced with uncertainty, pressure or conflict.

Indicators
1 Gives self time to think and respond.

2 Recognizes own needs, wants as important.
3 Does not accept put-downs or rejection by others.
4 Gives self-recognition and accepts recognition from others.
5 Accepts and acknowledges own emotional feelings (e.g. anxiety) without being overwhelmed by them.
6 Does not put pressure on self or others to find the 'right' answer to a problem.
7 Is willing to try new approaches without being offered guarantees of the outcomes.
8 Does not put down other people, or their ideas.

Contra indicators
1 Interrupts own conversation or train of thought.
2 Puts self or own ideas down, e.g. 'This may be a silly idea'.
3 Looks continually to others for approval.
4 Avoids taking responsibility for self and others.
5 Passivity.
6 Hostility, blaming others, rejection.
7 Qualifies or justifies statements or actions, e.g. 'I did it this way because . . .'.
8 Says 'we', 'people', or 'one' rather than 'I'.
9 Over-polite, e.g. 'I wouldn't mind if you . . .'.

Each identified attitude or skill can be analysed in this way to facilitate assessment of the effectiveness of any programme.

Once the trainer has specified the learning aims—and for any programme of five days' duration more than five learning aims is bordering on the impossible—then he or she needs to identify what needs to happen in the group in order to achieve them. This may be referred to as setting *process* aims as distinct to *content* aims. Some typical process aims, which intend to develop a helping relationship within the group, may include—openness, trust, self-disclosure, support and challenge. And like the content aims each one of these process aims is likely to be more appropriate at different parts of the programme. For example, most people are happier about giving and receiving feedback (i.e. challenge) after they have had an opportunity to talk about themselves (i.e. self-disclosure). Similarly, most people are happier about talking of themselves as people after they have spoken about the nature of their jobs. Trainers who do not work with a clear picture of the process aims are unlikely to manage the risk level effectively with the inevitable consequence that individuals will marshal their resistances to take care of themselves.

At an early stage in the setting of aims and programme design the trainer would be well advised to talk to members of the target population. A good structure for such talks is to offer a preliminary statement of aims and an outline programme and to gain reactions and suggestions from potential learners. As well as providing this kind of information the talks also provide important data about previous training, attitudes to the programme, and the differences between individuals. At a process level it also offers a clear message about the potential relationship between the trainer and learner being one of co-operation and mutual problem-solving. It is also an opportunity for the trainer to begin the process of offering him- or herself as a person as well as a professional.

Group size and composition

Most internal trainers are often under real pressure to increase the size of their groups on the grounds of cost effectiveness. Many managers, not surprisingly, are unaware of the consequences of mathematical progression on important group management issues like safety, risk, and sufficient air-time for individuals. On straight knowledge-based programmes it would appear that the task of providing information to 15 people is no different from providing the same information to an audience of 25 or 35. Such an assumption is only tenable, however, if the person has no expectation that people will be able both to retain the information and learn from the experience. If you doubt this caveat simply reflect on your experiences of attending lectures in school or university. Once the overriding imperative of sitting examinations has been met most learners are likely to experience a mental bowel movement within a short period of time. In the context of effective learning and change there is a need to chew over and assimilate information so that the learner can form clear gestalts of meaning. This presupposes a group size in which individuals feel safe enough to ask questions of the trainer, have an opportunity to discuss in small groups (of, say, 5–8), and have an opportunity to work with the information, either in the context of their own experiences or via a case-study.

Programmes which are concerned with changing attitudes or acquiring new skills pose even more critical problems in this respect. People need not only time and space in which to learn, they also need time and safety in which the group can learn *how* to learn with each other. As a rough guide on appropriate group size for these kinds of programmes my experience leads me to the formula given in Figure 3.1.

Programme length	No. of trainers	Group size
1 day	1	max. of 10
2–3 days	1 or 2	max. of 10
4–5 days	2	max. of 12

Figure 3.1 *Group size*

Whenever the size of group has exceeded these limits the learning situation has been unnecessarily imperilled for both the trainer(s) and the learners. The difficulty always, under these circumstances, is that of forming a helping relationship.

Group size is obviously related to that of composition, i.e. who is in the group. In this respect, the trainer is likely to be met with one of three types:

1 The stranger group—the individuals do not know each other, and are unlikely to meet in the normal course of their work.

2 The cousins group—the individuals do not work closely together, but already have some relationship with each other and are likely to have work contact in the future.

3 The family group—the individuals work together now and will in the future. Their relationships are not only work-based but are also likely to be social.

With both 'cousins' and 'family' groups the immediate focus of the group will be their relationship with each other. Their relationship with the trainer will always be secondary, and if he or she steps out of line—by raising the risk level too quickly, for instance—is always likely to be excluded or be managed by the group. With stranger groups, by contrast, their main focus of attention will be on their relationship with the trainer. Each member of the group will be looking for important information, including:

• What kind of person are you?
• Can you be trusted?
• Are you credible?
• What experience or qualifications do you have?
• Are you fair and honest?
• Are you genuine?

This information will be sought explicitly or implicitly at an early stage. The trainer who misreads this interest as a challenge, or assumes that to be trusted is his or her birthright, or attempts to project some kind of image or professional persona, is likely to have either a difficult time or have a relationship based on distance.

Although the process issues will vary with the composition of the group (with 'family' or 'cousins' groups the relationship with the trainer will emerge when basic issues of how to deal with each other have been clarified) the above formula for group size still holds good. The only modification would be for 'family' groups where I believe one trainer rather than two, irrespective of length of programme, is a more effective choice. The reason for this is that an important role for the trainer with such groups is to act as an umpire, an impartial but consistent regulator of rules. Two trainers, in this respect, can be confusing or contradictory, and such responses—particularly with team-building events—can make members of the group feel unsafe.

Designing the programme

A good programme, like a good play, should have three clear phases: a beginning, a middle, and an end. In broad terms, the beginning should be concerned with establishing relationships and a method of working; the middle is the task of working effectively together; and the end is concerned with closing down the relationship and assisting the return to work. It is worth looking at these three phases in some detail.

The beginning

Allowing for any preparation—like interviewing members of the target population—then the beginning of any programme starts with the first act of contact between the trainer and the learner. This contact might be vicarious—receiving joining instructions and programme, the learner arriving at the training room or centre; or direct—a pre-course telephone call or conversation or an informal welcome over coffee on the first day of the programme. Whether vicarious or direct the trainer needs to be aware that, as in any other context, first impressions can be powerful and are always important. One danger facing all trainers is that of becoming blasé or preoccupied at the start of programmes. Failure to recognize that the learner is having to cope with a lot of uncertainty—the nature of the programme, joining a new group, being on unfamiliar territory, not knowing how to behave—and is looking for a minimum of guidance and support, can set back the individual and the group in the first twenty-four hours. This will almost inevitably mean that the trainer has to work hard to recover the position.

It is also worth paying attention to the impact of environmental issues, like the layout of the training room (e.g. a formal arrangement of table and chairs is likely, intentionally or not, to convey a message of formality about the nature of the programme and of how to behave). Similarly, the style of dress and manner of greeting will support or contradict that message. The situation is analogous to that of arriving at a party and not knowing how to behave. A guest, under these circumstances, will be looking to the host or hostess for clues on how to behave. Once those clues have been received the guest is then able to enjoy the party. I have worked with other trainers who have made a point of not being helpful in this way, and have argued that people's responses to uncertainty is a useful source for learning. Having attended a number of courses myself as a learner I have experienced the difference between being hosted in this way and being 'encouraged' to learn, and I find the latter disrespectful and an obstacle to learning. How can I trust someone to help me learn if they do not have the sensitivity to welcome me into their home?

Moving beyond the point of first contact and on to the start of the programme there are some important activities that need to be carried out. In order, these are: administration, introductions, and nature of the programme. Offering administration details is the formal part of the hosting role: letting the group know where the toilets are, the approximate time and nature of breaks. Any restrictions on the use of the premises, takes away some potentially irritating uncertainty. The format for the introductions is variable—introduce yourself or your partner; the choice of required information (about job, learning needs, expectations of the programme, personal information) should reflect the nature of the programme. For example, on programmes which contain a significant amount of personal-awareness work then the choice of questions should be biased towards more personal statements. Or, on influencing-skills programmes, for instance, learners should be requested to talk about themselves rather than to introduce a partner. Whatever the chosen format it is advisable for the trainer(s) to introduce themselves in the same way in response to the same questions.

There appears to be a tendency for trainers to rush through introductions, reducing the activity to a necessary ritual. My own experience is that the way the trainer handles the introductions—too speedy, too slow, as a ritual or a gimmick—will set a climate that may need to be reset twenty-four hours or so into the programme. If he or she is too fast and controlling, for instance, it could encourage passivity (the undeclared assumption being that the trainer is in charge). If the trainer demonstrably does not listen, or makes jokes at people's expense, or is disinterested in what delegates say, then the group is likely to feel that it is an unsafe place to learn. There was a fashion for a number of years, and still survives in some places, for the trainer to introduce an 'ice-breaker', i.e. some lighthearted activity to help people feel at ease. Some examples of which I have been on the receiving end are: to draw a picture; walk round the room smiling at people; being asked to dance; and various relaxation exercises. Often the reactions to such ice-breakers has been the opposite of what was intended, i.e. a severe case of frost-bite develops. Such activities can leave bad feelings around for some time.

Information about the nature of the programme—not the content—should offer some clear guidelines about the nature of the learning process (e.g. the balance between theory, discussion, activities, workshops); any unifying model that underlies the programme (e.g. working through the cycle of awareness—choices—experimentation—decisions); a statement about whether what happens in the group is confidential or not; whether people are expected to take notes or whether handouts will be provided; and any expectations the trainer might have about the responsibility for learning. Additionally, at this point, I also offer some ground rules for learning on programmes which aim to change skills or attitudes. According to the programme, such ground rules may include prescription (e.g. how to give and receive feedback) and permission (e.g. it's OK to make mistakes, to do a bad job, be confused or uncertain etc.). Always, one important ground rule is that members of the group can add their own suggestions to the list which is put on flipchart paper and posted in the room. The purpose of such ground rules is twofold: one, to provide a common understanding of how to behave (thus meeting some of the needs for safety); and, two, actively to share the responsibility for learning, by inviting them to set their own rules.

The middle

As soon as the introductory activities are over the main body of the programme (what I describe as the middle) begins. There is a cliché used by trainers about 'the need to start where the group is'. Despite paying lip-service to this adage many trainers do not act upon this good advice. Instead, they have a tendency to launch into theory or some structured learning activity designed to open a key learning area in the programme. So, for example, the start of a counselling-skills programme may well include offering definitions of counselling, or some skills exercise (e.g. listening). In choosing to follow the adage, then, a better option would be to split the course into small groups and then ask them to define what counselling is, and to identify the core skills of counselling. Their reports will provide the trainer with invaluable information about the levels of knowledge and skills within the group. It will also quickly provide evidence of views and values (about people, organizations, responsibility) which if not aired at this stage may need to be prised out at a later stage. For example, many people in organizations have a belief that personal problems (i.e. non-work) should not be raised at work, and should not be tackled by an in-house counsellor.

Unless this issue is raised explicitly and early then an individual with this belief is going to be at a severe disadvantage if the rest of the group and the trainer operate with a different belief.

A major consideration in designing the structure of any programme is that of risk. It is a term that I have already used in this book when describing the process of resistance (p. 32 *et seq*.). The experience of feeling at risk is likely to vary from person to person but is most certain to arise when:

- an individual takes some action and does not know what the outcome will be;
- an individual believes that he or she lacks the resources to cope with a situation.

The range of conditions on any programme where the above can occur are numerous, and can include: introducing yourself or your partner; reporting back on a small-group discussion; asking questions in a large group; taking part in a group exercise or role play; and any feedback activity. Most trainers are aware of risk situations on skills and attitudinal programmes, but it is too easy to assume that what we may see as safe programmes (knowledge-based) or safe parts of programmes can be experienced as high-risk by some learners. One of the problems, in this respect, is that not only is the experience of risk subjective, but also the ways in which we cope with risk are also unpredictable. Such ways may include:

- passivity
- expressing fear, caution and concern for others rather than for self
- expressing confusion or lack of understanding
- asking detailed questions or for clarification
- cynicism or hostility
- suspicion or withdrawal
- discounting experiences or compulsive joking
- acting tough or being insensitive
- sarcasm

Although the trainer cannot totally control the risk level in the group there are three design factors that directly affect the level at any one time. These are: size of group, variety of learning experience, and the time focus of the learning experience. In looking at these factors I would like to start with the latter.

Time focus   Activities which concentrate on what is happening now within the group (*here-and-now*) are always high risk. The simplest kind of here-and-now activity involves Person A giving feedback to Person B about what he or she is doing now. A lower-risk option would involve giving feedback on what happened in the recent past, as when reviewing a learning activity. This *there-and-then* focus provides the learner with appropriate escape routes if he or she so needs them (e.g. 'I am not normally like this', or, 'That's not really me on the close circuit TV monitor'). An even safer option is to focus on what people have done in the past or will do in the future. Both these time frames are there-and-then but provide greater escape routes because no one in the group has had experience of the talker's behaviour in those circumstances. Simply by being aware of this factor the trainer can structure the design of the programme so that there-and-then activities precede any forays into here-and-now. Such a design provides a structure of increasing risk.

Size of group   In choosing activities the trainer always has options about the size of particular groups to carry out the tasks. These can range from individual work, pairs, trios, quartets up to full group. There are very few training activities around that cannot be modified in this way—though listening and feedback exercises do obviously require a minimum of two people. A simple rule of size is that the larger the group the higher the risk.

Variety of learning experiences   Irrespective of the kind of programme the variety of kinds of sessions that can be used is large. They range from theory inputs, large group and small-group discussion, case studies, organization simulations, role plays, structured learning experiences for individuals, pairs, trios and other sizes of groups. The design of any programme should include a variety of these experiences but the trainer needs to be aware of the contrasting dangers of either being locked into one kind of learning experience or of switching the methods with each sessions. Both of these dangers are likely to be experienced on skills programmes. As an example of the former, I attended some years ago a training of trainers programme which was structured on the simple basis that each participant would either be running a training session or be a learner in a colleague's session. At the end of each session the 'trainer' would receive detailed feedback from the trainers and the participants. By Wednesday morning of this five-day programme each one of us was suffering high levels of performance anxiety, and one member of the group was so distressed that he stormed out of the room during a colleague's session.

Similarly, to be on the receiving end of a programme that shifts alarmingly from role-play to case study to instrumented learning to here-and-now feedback activities also creates problems with risk levels because there is simply not enough time for people to integrate their learning experiences and so they accumulate unfinished situations from each new activity. Such programmes are ticking bombs of bad feelings.

In general terms the model of increasing risk is a good design option but the trainer needs to be aware of the danger which can occur when a group reaches a level of intensity in which they become stuck in here-and-now activities of great emotionality. I use the term 'hot housing' to describe this situation. At first sight it might appear a desirable state to achieve—people are learning and changing—but the costs can be considerable, e.g. exhaustion; an unwillingness to let go of the programme and other course members, and depression when the programme is over. If such a state appears to be imminent the trainer is well-advised to change the learning experience, e.g. theory input, relaxation exercises, time-out for reflection or rest.

Because the trainer cannot totally control the risk level there is always likely to be times, on any programme, when a learner hits a crisis of risk—what I have earlier described as an impasse (see p. 33). Some useful options for a trainer in these circumstances include:

- give permission for the learner to do what he or she needs to do (e.g. talk, be silent, be ignored etc.);
- give the learner permission to express feelings (sadness, anger, doubt etc.) by saying 'It's OK to cry/be angry' etc.;
- offer protection, e.g. putting arm around him or her;
- encourage the learner to look slowly round the group or to make eye contact with whoever he or she feels safe with (this is particularly important if the learner feels ashamed);
- encourage the learner to take some deep breaths;
- encourage the person to think about what they need now;
- remain silent;
- ask the group to leave the person alone for a specified period of time;
- change the focus of attention;
- wait until the end of the session and offer appropriate support.

The best option, always, is to ask the learner what he or she wants and to act on their direction. Apart from the learner the trainer needs also to consider the reactions of other members of the group. A common response to an individual's crying is for other members of the group to feel uncomfortable and to look for someone to blame—usually, the trainer. When the immediate crisis is over, and the needs of the learner have been seen to, it is advisable to ask each member of the group how they are feeling. The purpose of this is not only to bring to the surface any anger or blame but also to check whether someone else in the group is feeling distressed in response to what has occurred. This is particularly important with all-male groups when the incidence of one person crying can trigger off similar unfinished business for others.

The end The closure of any programme is likely to contain a number of different endings. Principally it includes, the need to close down a particular learning process; the need to close down the special relationships which have enabled the learning to take place; and, a need to reorientate the learners to the workplace.

The time required for effective closure can be considerable. For example, on a five-days skills or attitudinal progamme I would view the end of Thursday afternoon as the beginning of that period, and would be resistant to introducing any significant learning experience from then on. By significant I would include any new ideas or concepts, skills or personal learning. Instead I use the time for reflection and consolidation of what has taken place. Whatever the nature of the programme the closure needs to be concerned with thinking, reflection and forward planning, and to provide whatever assistance individuals may need to close down any unfinished situations that have emerged during the week. Any format of back-home planning activity is the best vehicle for ensuring this takes place. Although it is foolish to expect that all the learning needs have been met and that people have total clarity about what has happened the trainer who attempts to keep pushing up to the course feedback session is doing a disservice to the group.

People also need time to say goodbye to those they have worked with, and generally it would appear that most of us have difficulty in managing this process effectively. It always appears easier to ignore the process or to hurry or depersonalize the activity. The result is that people often leave effective programmes with regrets about not saying what they wanted to, and then distracting themselves on the journey home with these regrets. To safeguard against this possibility I often allow an hour of programme time for people to say whatever they need to say so that they are ready to move on to the next situation.

Session design checklist

1 Set aims for the session
   • Identify no more than three learning points.
   • Are there also process aims (e.g. to develop trust)?

2 Structure of session
   • Need a beginning, middle and end.
   • What is the risk level?
   • Do you need handouts and equipment?

3 Beginning
   • Tell group the aims, methods and timings.
   • Put into context of programme.
   • Explain the role of facilitator.

4 Middle
   • Activity in pairs, small group, large group?
   • Any ground rules?
   • Will there be a formal or informal feedback to the large group?
   • A spokesperson for small groups, open discussion of all individuals to make statements?

5 End
   • Structured or unstructured review?
   • Log contributions on flipchart or overhead projector?
   • Do you respond to, or build upon, their contributions?
   • Do you lead to, or add theory on to, the review?
   • Summarize what has happened.
   • Tell them what happens next.

Running a session

Within the context of any programme there are some useful guidelines for running a session. One of the earliest pieces of advice given to me on this topic was 'Tell them what will happen, tell them what is happening, then tell them what happened'. The virtue of this advice is most obvious when the trainer is on the receiving end of someone else's programme and is surprised to find that the purpose and structure is not always as apparent to the learner as it is to the trainer.

A later piece of advice, which complements the former, was 'Be yourself—forget about being a trainer'. The art of talking simply and clearly with, and not at, people, seems to be absent from the content of most presentation-skills programmes. Trainers I have worked with who have been on such programmes appear controlled and stilted and phobic about 'intrusive' non-verbal behaviour. All their energy and awareness is turned in upon themselves—and they do not see or respond to what is happening in the group.

In addition to the above some other guidelines on running a session are:

1 Have a clear content aim—but only one per session. If it is a theory input keep it simple. See the following section on group development: the text is slightly more than I would cover in a session lasting 1½ hours.
2 Does the session have a particular process aim? Such an aim might be to encourage discussion in the large group or to encourage self-disclosure in small groups.
3 Outline the structure of the session to the group and make clear your expectations of them, e.g. 'I want one of you to report back on your answers to these questions'.
4 All briefings should be written on handouts or flipcharts.
5 Specify what your role will be during small-group work and in the large group.
6 If the session is structured on the basis of an introduction, activity, and review, be clear about the structure of the review.
7 When conducting the review decide whether (a) you intend to summarize their contributions; (b) you will add to or build on their contributions; (c) you will lead into appropriate theory.
8 At the end of the session tell the group how this fits into the rest of the programme and offer a link to the next session.

Not least, pay attention to ways in which you can take of yourself. They may include: speaking slowly; taking deep breaths; working in a way you feel comfortable (e.g. standing, walking, sitting); preparing material beforehand; slowing down; keeping eye contact with individuals; and if you do not know the answer to a question then say so!

Common faults

One of the big problems facing all new trainers is that they attempt *too* much of everything. Whether this is a response to uncertainty or a desire for perfection is unclear but what is apparent, however, is that the attempt is self-defeating. Groups on the receiving end of a trainer who attempts to cover *too* much material or offers *too* much complexity or goes *too* fast or promotes *too* much intensity will invariably say goodbye to him or her at an early stage in the programme. The trainer, on the other hand, who sees his or her role to be one of responding to the needs of the group through observing and listening will be promoting one side of the helping relationship. One important remedy to guard against these dangers is to simply ask the group about these issues at appropriate times during the programme (for example, an end-of-day review structured simply on the basis of inviting everyone in turn, including the trainer, to make some statement about their level of satisfaction). Such questions not only offer guidance at a content level but at a process level they help to establish a relationship of equality of influence.

Group development

The trainer needs to be aware that when new groups are formed there is an important process, analogous to the one we experience as individuals, which will shape the development of the group and influence the quality of learning and change. According to Schein[1] this process is stimulated by each group member looking for answers to the following questions:

- Who am I to be in this group?
- Will I be able to control and influence others?
- Will the group goals include my own needs?
- Will I be liked and accepted by the group?
- How close a group will we be?

The ability of individuals and groups to work through these issues—for rarely are these questions made explicit—will determine how far a particular group will develop in the course of its natural life. Assuming that these questions are adequately answered, then the group will move through the following stages.

Dependency

The normal starting position for most groups in which they look to the leader for safety, guidance, structure and support. Members of the group will follow any ground rules for behaviour, and if these are not made explicit by the leader then certain norms of behaviour will quickly develop (e.g. not interrupting others, especially the leader; being prepared to wait their turn to speak; not being disrespectful etc). These rules or norms are very important and serve the same kind of purpose as they do in organized sporting activities, i.e. to provide order, structure and safety. Playing by these common rules allows individuals to settle down and take stock of other members of the group. The usual expectation of the leader is that he or she will be impartial and fair to all, and if conflict should emerge the leader will take responsibility for managing the process.

Counter-dependency

When individuals have met their basic needs for safety and are ready to move on to meeting their personal goals then there is also a willingness to raise conflict with other members of the group. This will be accompanied by a readiness to modify or break the original ground rules or norms (e.g. members will interrupt each other; start challenging the authority of the leader). Tuckman[2] describes this stage as 'storming', and it can be a stormy episode in the life of a group with individuals radically changing their pattern of behaviour (e.g. low contributors becoming high contributors). This stage is often marked by the emergence of sub-groups or pairings and can lead, critically, to polarization within the group. The nature of the conflict that emerges at this stage is characterized by the assumption that I can only meet my needs at the expense of yours.

Cohesion

When this conflict has been successfully worked through there is a more equitable sharing of responsibility for what happens in the group, and a clear sense of belonging to a team. Roles, objectives and methods are clarified or defined for the first time and basic leadership and membership issues have been resolved. The new norms that emerge at this stage are likely to be explicit rather than implicit. Everyone starts deferring to the 'group', e.g. 'If the group will allow me to . . .'; 'if the group is happy about . . .'. This abstraction of the 'group' can be tyrannical with individual members policing the boundaries of acceptable behaviour and they will reprimand anyone showing disloyalty to the group. It is usually at this stage in their development that the group undertakes every social activity as a 'group'—refreshment and meal breaks, late-night drinking or other activities—and individuals seek permission from the others not to attend. It is as if there is a shared, but unspoken, assumption that the cohesiveness of the group will be shattered by the absence of individual members. Similarly, certain 'rites of passage' can be demanded of individuals in the training room, e.g. everyone is expected to make some disclosure about themselves; or to undertake some intense learning experience; or to take the lead in some learning activity like a role play.

Interdependence

The last stage of development takes place when the 'tyranny' of group membership has been replaced by a willingness to allow individuals to set their own limits within the training room and during social time, i.e. they are allowed to learn at their own pace and in their own time; they are also allowed to be present or absent from group activities. This change takes place when people realize that the effectiveness of the group is enhanced, and not endangered, by individuals exercising responsibility for their own needs.

I said at the start of this description of group development that the process is analogous to that which we experience as individuals, and indeed these four stages can be equated to childhood (dependency), adolescence (counter-dependency), cohesion (early adulthood), and maturity (interdependence). The fact that in terms of personal development individuals can get stuck in one of these stages (e.g. the person always dependent on leadership and guidance from others; the 'rebel'; and the person who will only act on the basis of full agreement from his or her peer group) is paralleled at the group-process level. Many training groups become locked into dependency, counter-dependency or cohesion, and the kind of relationship offered by the trainer is a major determinant of this blockage. The trainer who adopts an instrumental relationship with a group through over-control or abdication is encouraging this to happen.

The trainer who adopts the helping relationship is more able to help the group to work through the four stages, because he or she assumes (1) that they are a member of the group—albeit with a special role; and (2) by offering a relationship of equal influence they are helping to bring to the surface the important process issues of control, influence, liking and acceptance that Schein has identified as being central to the membership of every group. By being willing to look at these issues for himself or herself the trainer is 'modelling' the kinds of behaviour that individuals need to develop an effective group. If I as a trainer demonstrably allow myself to influence and be influenced by you as a group member then I am also offering you a model of a relationship that you can use, to similar effect, with other members of the group.

Co-training

It is axiomatic, but worthy of repetition, that where two or more trainers are involved in running a programme their effectiveness as a team will depend on (1) a shared understanding of the aims and content; (2) a common approach or style when working with the group; (3) a relationship based on professional respect. Having worked with numerous trainers over the years I realize that whatever disparities between members of a training team—experience, knowledge, skills, models, beliefs etc.—the major factor that will determine their effectiveness as a team is their willingness to respect and accept each other as people *and the differences between them*. Where this respect and acceptance is lacking, the team and the group with which they work will suffer. What inevitably impedes the development of this personal respect is a failure to acknowledge that training—like other performance activities, e.g. acting, musicianship, therapy etc.—is a narcissistic profession. What I mean by narcissistic is that the product 'sold' by the trainer is himself or herself, and that this product is explicitly and regularly assessed by others. The nature of this assessment is a simple one—on the one hand approval, on the other rejection. Many trainers find it difficult to cope with this continuing process of being 'accepted' and 'rejected' by groups. Rather than deal with this problem explicitly, trainers have a tendency to displace this concern by projecting it on to their colleagues, i.e. if I can find some fault in my colleague then I can 'blame' him or her, explicitly or implicitly, for any failure of the programme. Or I may choose to find fault with the design of the programme instead of facing my repressed concerns or disquiet about being assessed myself. This displacement is often triggered when one trainer receives a lot of appreciation from a group and his or her colleague received none or little. The co-training relationship naturally lends itself to repressed and unacknowledged feelings of inadequacy and envy. I have attended a number of post-course sessions where the training team have offered each other feedback about their performance on a programme where the 'helpful' negative feedback to a colleague has spoken more about the hidden agenda of the giver than it has about the behaviour of the receiver.

The unacknowledged process issue that often arises is that of competition between trainers. When this issue is acted out in the training room groups have a great ability to form their own judgements about the credibility of both trainers, and may choose to engage in the process by playing off one trainer against the other.

Despite this, the one question that teams of trainers will avoid dealing with is 'Who is the best trainer in this team?' Such a question will be met with rationalization, hostility, or embarrassment, despite the fact that each member of that team would be willing to acknowledge their concerns and doubts about being an effective trainer. Teams that are willing to deal openly with the question are the ones most likely to develop the personal respect required to offer an effective helping relationship to a group.

Summary In this chapter I have looked at some of the prevailing organizational attitudes to training, and how these are likely to affect both the trainer and the training programme. I have then described how the design and management of programmes can assist the development of the helping relationship. In addition to discussing a range of tactical decisions (about programme aims, group size and composition, and the structuring of both programmes and individual sessions), I have also described how an understanding of the stages of group development is crucial to managing effective learning. Finally, I have looked at some of the key issues which can adversely affect the co-training relationship.

In the next chapter I will look at the helping relationship in counselling.

References
1. Edgar Schein, *Process Consultation* (Addison-Wesley, 1969).
2. B. Tuckman and M. Jensen, 'Stages of Small Group Development Revisited', *Group and Organization Studies* (1977), 419–27.

The Milk Marketing Board: influencing-skills programme

There are three main reasons for choosing this programme as a case study for this book:

1 It is a short (5-days) skills programme.
2 The programme has been run many times (approx. 20), and has consequently been modified over the years.
3 It is one of the first—if not the first—programmes to be provided for one organization which is explicitly based on the Gestalt approach.

Need identification

I was first approached by the internal training officer of the Milk Marketing Board in the autumn of 1982 to design and run the programme. The population for the programme was clearly defined; they were to be drawn from members of the Graduate Entry Training Scheme. During the twelve months of their training programme members were already attending a number of programmes, some provided in-house, others by external training agencies. Of the programmes currently provided the nearest in content and approach was a five-day 'personal development programme'. This programme provided an introduction to some management skills, e.g. communication, working in groups, creativity, and was designed and tutored by an external training agency.

It was felt that a programme in influencing skills was required to meet the need for assertiveness and creativity at that particular level in the organization. Some important factors specified for the desired programme were (1) the use of Gestalt as the basic model for developing understanding and skills in assertiveness; and (2) there should be no overlap of the content with the existing 'personal development programme'. The internal trainer would also co-tutor on the new programme.

Preliminary analysis

As the first step in the design process there were a number of interviews held with members of the target population. In addition, the internal trainer sought the views of some managers who had experienced supervising those who had already emerged from the management training scheme. Both the target population and the managers confirmed the soundness of the initial diagnosis and agreed that such a training programme should be included.

Design issues

In terms of designing the programme a number of important issues began to emerge. One, the membership of each year's entry to the scheme would go through a number of learning events *together*. Therefore, by the time they attended this programme the group would already have established an identity among themselves, and would naturally be inclined to look on the trainers as 'outsiders'. Two, their experience of working in an organization would be limited.

For these two reasons, the decision was made to offer this programme as near to the end of the second year of their organizational life as possible.

From the trainer's viewpoint the design needed to embrace the following criteria:

1 To ease the group into a different way of learning, and to pass responsibility over to them as soon as possible for managing their personal learning needs.
2 To base the learning on what little organizational experience they do have.
3 To give each individual as much 'air-time' as possible—to look at and work on the issue of confidence.
4 To give much more emphasis to skill practice at the expense, if need be, of theory.

An important feature of the programme was an agreement that the development of influencing skills should be based on increasing levels of personal awareness rather than offering groups set menus of skills. The learning cycle to be used would consist of:

• increasing self-awareness
• identifying new choices of behaviour
• experimenting with the new choices
• making decisions about the future use of these choices

Although an individual may go through this cycle a number of times during the week the structure of the programme would embody this cycle:

Monday—awareness
Tuesday—identifying choices
Wednesday/Thursday—experimentation
Friday—decision-making

The potential problem of the trainer being seen as an 'outsider' and threat to a cohesive group was to be accounted for by providing as much opportunity as possible to move easily into 'here-and-now' experiences as a vehicle for dealing with these issues (see pp. 45–46).

The programme

The pilot programme took place in February 1983, and the number of participants was limited to ten. A brief description of the programme currently provided is given below.

Monday
10.00   Arrival/coffee/administration
10.15   Introductions (standard introductions of name, job title etc., but also included is the question: 'Three people who have influenced me are . . .')
Nature of the programme (includes input on personal learning cycle of: awareness—choices—experimentation—decisions)
11.15   *Influencing at work*
Definitions and personal experiences of influencing at work (small group exercises to identify styles of influencing)
1.00   Lunch
2.00   *Influencing at work*
Input on model of influencing (small group exercise to explore different strategies)
3.45   Tea
4.00   *The nature of influencing*
Exercise and group discussion (each person evaluates their current ability on core skills of influencing e.g. listening, observing others, feedback etc.)
6.00   Close

Tuesday
9.15   *Influencing skills*
Opportunity to practise some core skills through small-group exercises
1.00   Lunch
2.00   *Assertive behaviour*
Theory input and small-group exercise
4.00   Tea
4.15   *Personal stocktaking*
Each course member asked to identify one personal-learning need for the workshop. (The need may be defined in terms of a particular behaviour, e.g. 'saying no to demands from others'; a particular skill, e.g. interpreting someone's behaviour; or, in terms of a particular situation, e.g. dealing with a difficult individual)
4.45   *Workshop*
Allocating about 45 minutes per person and constructing an appropriate learning event to meet their need
6.00   Close

Wednesday
9.15   *Workshop (contd)*
As above
1.00   Lunch

2.00 *Workshop (contd)*
      As above
4.00 *The organization and influencing*
      (Working in two groups participants are asked to make a presentation about the culture of the Milk Marketing Board, and to identify those factors which help and hinder their effectiveness at work)
6.00 Close

Thursday 9.15 *Managing uncertainty*
      Increasing personal effectiveness through managing anxiety and the development of confidence (this session includes Gestalt theory and Gestalt-based exercises to develop confidence)
1.00 Lunch
2.00 *Workshop*
      Completion of outstanding workshop activities
6.00 Close
7.00 Course dinner

Friday 9.15 *Personal learning review*
      Individual work on personal learning gains from the programme
9.45 *Managing effectiveness*
      Input and group discussion on methods for maintaining personal effectiveness at work
10.45 Coffee
10.30 *Back-home planning*
      Small-group counselling sessions on the development of action plans for work
12.00 *Course review*
12.45 Close of programme

Comments

Since the first programme in 1983 the content has been modified by experience and feedback. The nature of those changes—as shown in the programme above—have been (1) to increase workshop time at the expense of theory and exercises; and (2) to spread the workshop across three days. The major benefit of the latter is to allow those group members who may feel particularly vulnerable more time to develop their levels of self-support.

Because the design is heavily biased to the development of individual learning, and includes many opportunities to work in the 'here-and-now', the anticipated problems of the trainer being excluded or 'managed' by the group can be dealt with if, and when, they arise.

In 1986 the Milk Marketing Board decided to ask me to redesign the 'personal development programme' which members of the Graduate Entry Training Scheme attend twelve months before the 'influencing-skills programme'. This decision made it easier to ensure that there was no content overlap between the two programmes, and that some of the concepts introduced into the former (e.g. basic Transactional Analysis theory) could be reinforced, as appropriate, in the second programme.

CASE STUDY TWO

W H Smith Ltd: management development programme

Apart from being a distinct contrast to Case Study One, the reasons for including this programme are:

1 The length of the programme (September 1985–July 1987).
2 The programme was designed to meet the particular needs of the five participants, and the details of each stage had to reflect how the needs changed over time.
3 The programme was equally concerned with developing knowledge, skills and attitudes.
4 In terms of design, handling and maintenance it is probably the most demanding and complex programme that I have ever managed.

Need identification

W H Smith Ltd provide a general management assessment centre (GMAC) for senior executives. The main aim of GMAC is to identify training and development strategies for individuals as part of the company's manpower succession planning. One outcome of GMAC is the provision of management development programmes or strategies for particular groups of staff. These programmes are based on the concept of the self-managed learning group rather than the conventional mangement education approach.

My first contact with the organization was the request on their part for me to attend the follow-up to the 1985 GMAC and to work with a group (1) to feedback their assessment from GMAC; and (2) to help the individuals identify detailed action plans for development. This activity took three days.

As a result of this involvement I was then asked by the company training manager to design and provide a management development programme for a group of five senior executives. The aims of the programme were:

1 To satisfy the individual training and development needs as identified by GMAC.

2 To develop an understanding of different learning styles and to encourage approaches to self-managed learning.

3 To develop an autonomous learning group. This embraced two sub-aims:

    (a) taking responsibility as a group to manage their own learning activities;

    (b) individuals within the group to take responsibility for helping other members to learn from them.

Apart from these agreed aims the other stipulation by the client was that the group should undertake a project which they should present to the managing director on completion of the programme. The project should address a business or organizational issue facing the company.

Preliminary analysis

As a result of the three-day activity with members of the group I was familiar with the content and aims of the GMAC. It also provided an opportunity for me to work closely with the participants of the projected programme and to have a lot of information about their responses to the GMAC. Each of the five members had worked with the company for many years and were feeling very dispirited by their performance and assessment by GMAC. Rather than see, as the company clearly intended, that the assessment was the beginning of a process of development, they were choosing to look upon themselves as failures. Their initial response to the proposed programme was mixed. It was very apparent from this time that some important process issues had to be managed and dealt with at the earliest opportunity otherwise the programme—whatever its virtue—would not be sustainable for two years.

Design issues

The issues arising from the design and provision of the programme were very complex. Some of the more immediately obvious concerns were as follows.

1 Whatever the commonality of need between the five members of the group there was also a lot of diversity.

2 The needs that were apparent at the start (September 1985) were almost certain to change during the two years.

3 To sustain this programme over time I needed to include two other colleagues to manage the programme.

4 Some of the areas of need (e.g. finance, marketing, economic trends etc.) could only be met by experts in these fields, but they would need to be told not only *what* was required but also *how* to provide it in the context of the overall learning aims. (During their career with the company each of the participants had attended a number of specialist training programmes.)

5 There was a need to provide continuity for both the group and the learning process. Essentially, this meant I had to exercise control over all the elements of the programme and to maintain contact with the group.

6 Some of the identified needs would have to be met by providing training and development activities for individuals outside the group.

The programme

The programme contained a number of elements which were intended to interrelate with, and reinforce, each other. These elements were:

1 Six three-day residential workshops for the group.
2 Preparatory work by participants before each workshop.
3 Attendance on specialist courses for individual members of the group.
4 Individual counselling/tutorial sessions with the three tutors.
5 A group project to run concurrently with the programme.

The following is a brief description of each of these elements.

The three-day workshops

Workshop 1   *Self-managed learning and the development of individual action plans* (26–8 November 1985)
The workshop covered: approaches to learning; group behaviour and development; feedback skills; performance assessment; individual action plans.

Workshop 2   *Situation analysis and the problem-solving cycle* (20–22 January 1986)
The workshop covered: situational analysis; problem-solving cycle; creativity techniques.

Workshop 3   *Financial management* (16–18 April 1986)
The workshop covered: basic accounting; interpreting financial statements; company acquisition; management information; business planning.

Workshop 4   *Managing relationships* (10–12 September 1986)
The workshop covered: presentations and exercises by members of the group on what they had learned from attendance on specialized programmes; analysis of personal learning needs and a self-directed workshop to meet those needs.

Workshop 5   *Marketing* (14–16 January 1987)
The workshop covered: case-study presentations by members of the group; principles of marketing; marketing techniques; organizational simulation.

Workshop 6   *Special needs* (1–3 April 1987)
The workshop covered: economic trends; report writing; preparation for project presentation.

Preparatory work

The preparatory work served at least three purposes: (1) to design the detail of the next workshop; (2) for individuals to direct their own learning; and (3) to provide continuity. As an example of the kind of tasks involved the following is what the group were asked to undertake before Workshop 5.

1 Complete a detailed questionnaire of terms used in marketing. [This was to enable the specialist tutor to gauge the level of their current understanding.]

2 Each member of the group to analyse and review the marketing strategy of a major competitor to W H Smith Ltd. [A written report had to be submitted to the tutor before the workshop, and each person had to make a presentation to the other members of the group during the workshop.]

External programmes

Three members of the group attended behavioural science programmes during 1986 and these experiences formed the basis of their presentation at Workshop 4.

Individuals counselling/ tutorials

Individual counselling/tutorial sessions were provided for each member of the group at their workplace in the first year. Apart from meeting the obvious purposes these sessions provided the tutors with an opportunity to experience the kind of working environments and pressures with which participants were dealing. In addition, I also attended two meetings of the group when they were planning their project.

The project

At the end of Workshop 2 the group were briefed as follows on the extended project.

The project will incorporate a detailed analysis of opportunities facing senior managers in W H Smith Ltd, and you will be expected to present your conclusions to the Managing Director on Friday, 17 July 1987.

The specific topic areas, project objectives and methods of inquiry and analysis will need to fall within the project outline above.

Additional guidelines are:

1 The project should provide you with opportunities to examine issues related to the areas of the programme (e.g. financial management, marketing, managing relationships etc.).
2 The methods of inquiry and analysis should provide you with an opportunity to explore and experiment with different approaches to problem-solving and learning.

During the course of the programme the group met a number of times—I attended two special meetings near the end—to plan, co-ordinate, and discuss the project.

Comments

Many of the anticipated process issues (e.g. disappointment, anger, loss of confidence etc.) were explored during Workshop 1 but it needed four months for the group, individually and collectively, radically to change their perceptions about the development process. By the last six months the energy, commitment and determination of the group were markedly obvious to all who had any form of contact with them. One of the important factors that they acknowledged as contributing to this change was the growing realization that it was 'their' programme, to be designed and managed in response to their wishes, and that the role of the trainer was to provide them with a service. My views, feedback and guidance to them were dealt with on its merits, and, in that respect, I was also a member of the learning group.

Because of the complexity of the programme there was an early concern that the different elements could be experienced as a set of discrete obstacles on the path to completion. In the event, each of these elements reinforced and supported each other, and the programme was actually experienced as a coherent and integrated whole.

The administrative demands of the programme were considerable, far in excess of any comparable kind of training that I have experienced. One reason for this, other than the length of the programme, was the need to co-ordinate the number of parties involved:

1 The group.
2 The tutorial team.
3 The company, which involved a number of contacts (e.g. training and development, career development, and various line managers).
4 The specialist tutors (e.g. on Workshop 6 three tutors were involved).

The nature of the closing activity—the presentation of the project to the managing director—was a particularly satisfying conclusion. (1) because a tangible outcome, i.e. the project, could be assessed. (2) because the content and the presentation of the project demonstrated the learning gains of the individuals and the group. (3) the commitment of the company to training and development was demonstrated by the presence of the managing director and other senior managers at the presentation.

4 The counselling relationship

Whatever the differences in approach and practise of training and development activities within organizations in the UK there appears to be a shared attitude—obviously with some exceptions—that such provision is of value to both employees and the organization. Even where the provision is minimal—restricted to certain kinds of training (e.g. professional and technical); or to certain categories of employee (e.g. senior management)—the organization is likely to have some kind of policy about their responsibility for training. By contrast, it is my continuing experience that very few organizations have such a clear attitude or policy to the provision of counselling for employees.

In some of the older companies, particularly those with a history of paternalistic management, there may be a welfare section or officer charged with a vague responsibility for helping employees. In many organizations, in my experience, the provision of counselling is seen to be one of the 'people responsibilities' of the personnel department, though *who* offers the service and *how* is not clearly defined. Often, the word 'counselling' is used, by managers and trainers, as some kind of option that can be exercised in the context of an appraisal interview or as part of a disciplinary process. Having experienced managers and trainers demonstrating their 'counselling skills' in this kind of context on training programmes it is patently clear that the concept of counselling is much abused. I have also worked for organizations where the mention of counselling, however defined, is viewed as a totally alien practice which has no place in organizational life.

Whatever the prevailing organizational attitude to counselling, I have yet to work in any organization as a manager, trainer or consultant, where I have not been approached to provide employee counselling. Similarly, there must be very few trainers who have never been approached to offer counselling by a course member or an employee of their organization. Whatever stance an organization adopts to counselling it is clear, to most trainers at least, that (1) the need for the service exists, and (2) that trainers are the people most likely to be approached to provide that service.

The fact that trainers are approached for counselling is not surprising. Most training programmes, to a greater or lesser degree, encourage participants to talk about work situations as part of the learning process. For many participants this is likely to be their first opportunity to talk in a non-threatening way about difficulties that they encounter at work. Once they choose to take that opportunity, and receive help and guidance, some participants see the move into a 'counselling relationship' as an obvious choice. (I use inverted commas here to signify that participants would be reluctant to use the term counselling to describe this activity. For them, 'a chance to talk about a problem', 'to ask for advice or assistance', or 'to receive further feedback', are the kinds of terms that they use.)

The avoidance of the word 'counselling', even in situations where it is requested and offered, indicates to me, at least, the negative connotations with which society generally views the activity. In short, this view would suggest that counselling is for the sick and inadequate. The person who asks for counselling is in danger of being defined in those terms. Similarly, the organization that permits or encourages counselling might be seen as making an admission that it is also sick and inadequate. Such views produce the cycle of avoidance.

The cycle of avoidance

A manager notices that a subordinate who has been working effectively suddenly becomes less reliable in completing tasks or meeting deadlines. He is uncertain when given new tasks; begins to be described as oversensitive to others, and appears to be preoccupied and introspective. The manager makes a deliberately low-key enquiry of the subordinate and is met by a denial or minimization of the problem. She decides to leave the person alone on the basis that paying attention may exacerbate the situation, and the subordinate's performance deteriorates. He produces low quality work; time-keeping becomes a problem; a pattern of minor illnesses develops, and there are disagreements and rows with colleagues. The manager now intervenes and tells him to start working properly and to pay more attention to the needs of his colleagues. As a result of this talk the relationship between them becomes strained, conversations between them fall into a pattern that neither can break out of. At some point the manager takes some remedial action—has a disciplinary/counselling interview; sends the subordinate on the training course; ensures that he works in isolation; or sets more stringent work targets and closely polices his performance. These, and similar actions, simply put more pressure on the subordinate, and become a further source of problems that he has to cope with. In *extremis*, the subordinate is dismissed or resigns.

What lies at the heart of this destructive pattern is avoidance of the problem, by both the subordinate and the manager. Many participants who are sent on programmes to be 'cured' are some way into this cycle. Under these circumstances, the participant arrives with resentment and armoured to resist learning and change, while the trainer is presented with the problem of how to develop a helping relationship with an individual who feels suspicious and hostile at any overture of 'help'.

Cycle of avoidance checklist
1 Employee's performance declines.
2 Employee denies that there is a problem.
3 Performance and behaviour deteriorates.
4 Manager takes some form of remedial action.
5 Disciplinary action, dismissal or resignation.

Definition

Before looking at the kind of relationship required to deal with this situation I think that it is important to define the concept of counselling. The British Association of Counselling define counselling as follows:

People become engaged in Counselling when a person, occupying regularly or temporarily the role of counsellor, offers and agrees explicitly to give time, attention and respect to another person or persons who will be temporarily in the role of client.

The task of counselling is to give the client an opportunity to explore, discover and clarify ways of living more resourcefully and towards greater well being.[1]

Within the context of this book I would choose to gloss the second paragraph of this definition in terms of helping the individual to learn and manage personal-change strategies which lead to more effective and satisfying outcomes.

What counselling *is* can best be described in the context of a typical situation. A manager asked me for counselling on a problem that she was experiencing with a subordinate. She described herself as possessing an informal management style and with an active concern to involve her staff in the decision-making process. The problem subordinate, a middle-aged woman, had worked always with a formal authoritarian style of management and deeply resented the change of direction. She felt that discipline was slack and that members of staff would take advantage of the new manager. More importantly, she refused to change her style and actively subverted the new manager. The problem that was initially posed by the manager to me was—what strategies could she use to change the behaviour of the subordinate?

Before the manager had approached me for counselling she had spoken to other people about the problem and had received a lot of advice and suggestions about how to proceed. The problem remained, and as long as it stayed defined in terms of how to change the subordinate so long it would remain. As soon as the focus switched to how the situation was a problem for the manager (her discomfort about being seen as 'hard' and 'wicked') then the appropriate choice of action became immediately obvious to her. Instead of trying to suppress her disapproval and anger and attempting to be 'reasonable' and 'understanding' to the subordinate, the acceptance of her true feelings enabled her to use a wide variety of behaviours in dealing with the situation. The process of counselling helped her to understand more about herself, in particular the ways in which she limited her behaviours through a denial of feelings.

Counselling is not primarily concerned with solving problems or seeking particular answers; it is about helping people understand more clearly how they are managing a situation, how they make things easy of difficult for themselves, and how they restrict their ability to solve problems. Answers to the problem should emerge from counselling but the nature of that answer can only be known by the client.

Models of counselling

Although the British Association of Counselling definition is the one most widely acknowledged in the UK it is also true that there is a wide variety of models and approaches available. This variety embraces not just a difference in techniques (e.g. use of role-play in Co-counselling and Psychodrama; talking to an empty chair in Gestalt) but also a difference in the counsellor–client relationship (e.g. the 'unconditional acceptance' of the counsellor in the Rogerian approach; the interpretative role in psychoanalysis). There are also differences in values between the different schools (e.g. the instrumented approach of Behaviour Modification compared to the post-Rogerian approach of Positive Affirmation). It is not my intention to say any more about the different schools. For the reader interested in gaining more information in this area I would recommend *Counselling Shop* by Brigid Proctor[2] as a useful guide.

The model that I use and find to be of most value is that of Gestalt, and what I have described in Chapter 2 see 'The helping relationship'—is the methodology of Gestalt counselling. I now intend to explore in more detail how this approach can form the basis of the counselling relationship.

The stages of counselling

Irrespective of the particular approach adopted by the counsellor (e.g. TA, Gestalt, Rogerian etc.), it is possible to see the counselling relationship as one which includes a number of important and recognizable stages. In any particular counselling relationship some of these stages may not be immediately obvious, may be dealt with very quickly, or may merge seamlessly into each other. However, problems are likely to arise if the counsellor does not deal adequately with the issues that shape the sequence of these stages. There are six different stages:

Stages of counselling

1 Establishing the contract
2 Establishing the relationship
3 Exploring the problem
4 Defining the problem
5 Identification of action
6 Closing the relationship

Establishing the contract

At the start there is a need to define some ground rules for the relationship. First, there needs to be an agreement between both parties that the counsellor and client are willing to offer these respective roles to each other. The trainer, for whatever reason (e.g. tiredness, competing priorities, dislike or lack of interest in the client etc.), may not want to assume the role of counsellor. This decision, particularly in the context of running a training programme, needs to be made positively. Equally, the client needs to make a positive decision that he or she wants to enter into the relationship. This is a particularly important consideration where the client could be meeting the counsellor on a regular basis in the normal course of work or social situations.

This decision is dependent on the counsellor being able to clarify what such a relationship will involve and what he or she is prepared to offer the client (e.g. time, listening, questioning, feedback, challenge etc.). The counsellor should also make clear what is not on offer (e.g. advice, solutions, taking sides). Part of the clarification should also involve a clear statement about the client's having responsibility for finding the answers and taking action. This enables the client, who may only be looking for advice or an opportunity to moan, to satisfy those needs elsewhere.

Second, there needs to be some procedural agreements. For example, the length of the session; whether this is the first in a number of sessions; and, importantly, how the counsellor will make him- or herself available to the client. The purpose of such agreements is to protect both parties from abuse. In the case of the counsellor these agreements protect against exhaustion and burn-out. For the client, there is protection against unmet expectations and disappointment.

Third, and most importantly, for the internal trainer, there needs to be a clear statement about the extent to which he or she can offer confidentiality to the client. The trainer who works for an organization is often expected to be involved in a number of responsibilities (e.g. assisting managers in appraisal, disciplinary, and promotion interviews) where he or she may be called upon to make judgements about employees. In some organizations, they may even be called upon to make assessments of employees' performance on training programmes. Even where such assessments are not formal, trainers are often approached by line managers, invariably senior to them in the hierarchy, asking for a 'discreet' word about someone who attended a recent programme. All these situations represent demands on the trainer to break confidentiality. The extent to which the trainer does choose to manage these conflicting demands needs to be stated clearly.

Too often, in my experience, this stage is managed badly, with the result that counselling degenerates into a mutually abusive relationship. On the one hand, the trainer can quickly burn out with exhaustion and attempting to reconcile conflicting organizational demands. On the other, the client can feel betrayed, used and rejected.

Establishing the relationship

Whatever the quality of the work or social relationship that exists between the two parties, the client will be looking for answers to some important questions about the counsellor. These questions may be summarized as:

- 'Who are you?' (i.e. what are you really like as a person?)
- 'Can I trust you?' (i.e. not only with the content of what I say, but also with my openness about myself)
- 'How will you respond?' (i.e. with disapproval, acceptance, superiority, rejection etc.)

The fact that the client chooses you as a counsellor does not mean that these questions have been answered; all it means is that he or she is willing to take the risk that you might offer acceptance, care and respect. The extent to which these questions are raised explicitly during counselling, either by the counsellor or client, is variable but they need to be answered to the satisfaction of the client.

Later in this chapter (see 'Experiences of counselling') I wish to include information about the client's perspective which illustrates this decision-making process.

Problem exploration

At the start of most counselling interviews the client is unlikely to be either willing or able to present the 'real' problem. At one level the reason for this is self-evident—if the client had that degree of clarity then the problem would not exist. Most clients, in my experience, begin the session with offering a deluge of information—background detail about events and personalities, feelings, perceptions, motivations etc. The reasons for providing this torrent can be many:

- a desire to unburden the emotional and cognitive debris that they have accumulated over time
- a way of testing the counsellor (i.e. can he or she cope?)
- a desire to present the whole landscape in one go
- the client is confused or baffled
- the client is in distress
- the client is obsessed with detail as a way of avoiding the real problem
- the client wants to live with an unresolvable problem

This last reason may seem surprising, particularly if you find it hard to believe that any person who is clearly suffering, troubled, or in distress does not want to solve the problem. My experience is that such people do want to change the situation *but* only on the condition that everyone around them changes while they remain the same.

What is of special significance at this stage is not the *content* of what is offered but the *process* of how it is offered. The response of many counsellors is to treat this information like pieces of jigsaw—to systematically collect and order with a view to assemble the overall picture. Once the picture is complete, then the solutions become obvious. Rather than be seduced into this pastime a better option for the counsellor is to pay attention to his or her experiences of the client. First, how does the client speak: fast, slow or laboured? What feelings are being expressed or talked about? What non-verbal behaviours strike you as interesting, curious or odd, e.g.

- facial expressions?
- body posture?
- pattern of eye contact (sustained, avoided, broken)?
- gestures and body movements?

How do these behaviours reinforce or contradict the verbal statements? For example, making self-deprecatory statements and smiling. Last, but by no means least, how do you respond to him or her moment by moment (e.g. bored, interested, impatient, tired, breathless, confused, sad, concerned etc.)? All of this information that the counsellor has access to—and which is invariably outside the awareness of the client—is as important, if not more so, than the description of the problem.

By paying attention to, and offering, this information to the client several purposes are served:

1 It provides information that the client needs in order to have a clearer picture of themselves and the ways in which they are defining the problem and managing the situation.
2 It helps them to focus on how they contribute to the problem and what is the important issue in the situation.
3 The counsellor provides statements about he or she is responding, and goes some way to meeting the questions of the client raised in the previous section.

Problem definition   The move from exploration to definition will only take place when the client begins to take responsibility for their share of the problem. For example, the client receiving counselling on a problem relationship with a colleague will remain blocked while he or she persists in seeing the other as the source of the problem. Only when the client starts looking at their own behaviour and motivation in the situation will they be able to move forward.

The clues that this move to ownership of the problem is occurring is signalled at a number of levels:

Verbal   increasing use of words like 'I', 'me' or 'my' instead of 'him', 'her', 'them', 'one' or 'people'.
Non-verbal   intensity of body posture or gesture; general slowing down of movement and breathing pattern; increasing consistency between verbal and non-verbal behaviour.
Emotional   clearer statements and expressions of feelings.

What begins to emerge at a content level is a basic dilemma, e.g. do I stay or leave? do I take the risk of saying that I am angry or unhappy or do I continue to pretend? do I ignore the situation or take action? etc. Often when this point is reached the client has already discarded one choice (what he or she is doing at the moment) but may not be ready to move on. (This is the point of impasse, see p. 33). What may be required at this stage is rest, external support (especially receiving support from others), of the development of self-support systems (e.g. effective breathing and posture, acceptance of self, building confidence). There is a crucial need to safeguard against a precipitate movement into action which may be prompted by the client or the counsellor. If the process to this point has involved a significant amount of personal learning or an awareness of the existence of 'unfinished business' from previous relationships then choosing to stop for rest and integration is an advisable choice.

Identification of action   The choice of action by the client should be solely concerned with his or her behaviour and should not be directed at a particular response from others in the problem situation. So for example, the client's choice of making direct statements of his or her feelings to a colleague should not be selected with a view to that colleague's making some admission of guilt for past behaviour. The primary purpose of the new action is to give the client more choice and freedom in how to tackle the problem. The fact that the client has more freedom does offer an invitation for the other person to be different. For example, if their relationship has been characterized by a mutual blaming for difficulties the client's decision to stop blaming and to offer a joint problem-solving approach is likely to make it easier for the other person to stop blaming. But, and this is an important caveat, that other person may accept or reject the invitation. Despite whatever invitation is offered the colleague could well choose to remain the same. If the client can accept the possibility of the other's not changing then the new action is an appropriate choice for him or her.

In choosing the action the client should be able to identify a range of choices—from low- to high-risk. To stay with the example above, there is a range of how the feelings can be expressed. A low-risk option might be the statement:

'I'm concerned that every time we speak we very quickly start blaming each other. At such times I feel uncomfortable and angry. How do you feel?'

The highest-risk option, for both parties, could well involve full expression of anger. It is unlikely that such a choice—particularly if the client finds it difficult to express anger generally—would do more than make the speaker uncomfortable and exacerbate the situation.

The selected option is almost certainly to be some form of experimentation, and as such needs to be carefully managed. Some ways of managing are (a) to start with the low-risk option, and (b) to experiment with a low-risk person. Choosing to experiment with expressing anger, for instance, with the one person in the organization who is prone to excessive displays of anger is not a good choice.

Some of the ways in which the counsellor can offer support at this stage is to invite the client, in the comparative safety of the counselling relationship, to rehearse for the future. This may take the form of inviting the client to make statements of feelings as if the problem colleague were present. It might involve setting up a role play in which the counsellor acts as a stand-in for the colleague. Or it might involve inviting the client to criticize the counsellor for his or her behaviour, and in this way encourage the client to make statements of 'little angers'.

Closing the relationship   At some stage there will be a close to the counselling relationship, even if a different kind of work or social relationship continues to exist between the two parties. Whether the counselling was limited to one session, or several, there are a number of important issues that are worth paying attention to.

First, there is a need to summarize what has taken place. This serves two purposes: (a) to check if anything of importance has been 'lost', and (b) to provide a route map of the learning process for both parties.

Second, it is important to provide an opportunity for both parties to see if any unfinished business has accumulated in their relationship. This

Defining the problem   *Developing trust*

There are two main issues in any
counselling relationship:

1 The problem
2 The client's responsibility

The task of the counsellor is to
help the client clarify
and deal with both.

Resolving the problem   *Determining responsibility*

Tell me more about . . .   How do you feel about this?
Are you saying that . . .   What do you want?
What happens now?   How is this important for you?
How would you like to be different?   What do you expect of me?
Can you be specific?   What can you do?
What is your first step?

Figure 4.1 *Some basic questions for the counsellor*

may take the form of feedback, unsatisfied curiosity, appreciations, dis-
satisfactions, statements of learning.

Third, there should be clear statements about future actions, covering
not only the action steps of the client but also about the possibility of
resuming the counselling relationship.

It is important that this stage is managed carefully to avoid future
misunderstandings. It also serves to avoid the creation of dependency,
and not just that of the client on the counsellor. There is always the
danger that the counsellor can become dependent on the client to satisfy his or her needs—to be helpful, powerful, acceptable, respected etc.
The whole process of closure should be mutually managed. (Figure 4.1
above offers some basic questions for the counsellor).

The paradox of change

In my view the counselling relationship encapsulates and makes clear
some of the important dynamics of personal learning and change that
this book seeks to address. The process of managing personal learning
and change (whether the context be training or consultancy) is dependent upon establishing a helping relationship which is cleanly managed
(i.e. has a distinct beginning, middle, and end), is clearly in the interests
of the learner, and allows both parties to withdraw with a stronger
sense of personal power (i.e. more choices and freedom to manage
themselves and their environment).

Whatever the particular nature of the change strategy it is a product of
the client's need but it emerges from the interaction of the helping relationship.

What is also clearly obvious in the counselling relationship is the inherent paradox of change. This Zen Buddhist concept, which also lies at the heart of Gestalt therapy, can be expressed as follows:

> The more I try to be different the more I stay the same. I grow, develop, and change by becoming more of what I am.

It is fairly common for each of us to approach a learning event, counselling or training, with a clear agenda to be different, e.g. I want to be happy (not miserable); I want to be assertive (and not passive); I want to be confident (and not anxious). However, in spite of all my endeavours and wishes, at this moment I am miserable, passive or anxious; that is the reality. When I am able to accept myself for who I am (now) then I will be able to move on to the next moment and may be—happy, assertive, and anxious. One of the tasks of the counsellor is to offer that acceptance ('It's OK to be miserable') as a necessary precursor to the individual's being able to accept him- or herself.

The demand of self to be different, specifically or generally, is an introject (see p. 10) which has a pernicious effect on confidence, abilities and personal power. One of the recurring dangers facing any counsellor is to mirror that process either by pushing the client to be different, or by putting him- or herself under pressure to be different in some way (i.e. be more caring, helpful or effective). To watch a counsellor and client lock into this process, usually in pursuit of 'the answer', is like watching two boxers punch themselves into exhaustion.

Experiences of counselling

So far I have looked at counselling from the perspective of the counsellor. In a recent MA Dissertation *Counselling for Work*,[3] Ian McMonagle includes accounts by a number of people of their experiences of being counselled. These accounts, in words and pictures, present a remarkable consistency of experience. One account consists of a picture of the counsellor and client sitting on a free-floating cloud. In each corner of the picture the client has added the following words:

Me and my situation centre of attention.

What did it feel like?
Warm, useful, thought-provoking
Upsetting
Challenging
Comforting
Reassuring
Constructive

Absence
of competitiveness
of ego
of defensive routines
of deviousness

High-quality listening
Interest
Calm-gentle talking

McMonagle's comments on the picture are as follows:

[the picture] depicts an occasion by another individual who felt satisfyingly counselled and who found the scenario more easily expressed in words, however, again there is an underpinning support this time expressed as 'floating'. This scenario mentions what was absent and significantly that the individual's situation *and* the individual were the centre of attention, the vacuum suggesting that the counsellor was not bringing or working on their own agenda. Perhaps I read too much into the picture, but as with the other pictures there is not a clear view of who is helping who, no dominant person and, as the individual states, an absence of ego and competition . . . This picture also knocks firmly on the head that counselling is a soft option . . .

This and the other examples included closely match my experiences of being a client. The only addition that I would add to the above description is that I want the counsellor to be there and tangible but not to be intrusive. I also, as a client, want to be fully understood by the counsellor. This understanding does not involve approval, or even liking, but it does include acceptance.

It is my belief that anyone who takes up the role of counsellor (or indeed, trainer) needs continuing experience of what it is like to be on the receiving end. Without that experience it is too easy a danger to fall into an instrumental role, i.e. doing things to people at a distance. In addition to this danger, there is also the ethical issue of inviting people into an experience that the trainer has not been prepared to undertake for himself or herself. Apart from lacking the essential touchstone of experience (i.e. What are my anxieties about disclosing information about myself? What do I need when I hit the impasse? etc.), I am suspicious of trainers who do not practise what they preach. The nature of my suspicion is that such trainers use other people as a way of avoiding dealing with their own problems and concerns.

Formal and informal counselling

Within the organizational context I think that it is useful to draw a distinction between formal and informal counselling. For the reasons that I mention earlier in this chapter the concept of counselling tends to be an anathema in many organizations. The possibility of an employee entering into a formal counselling relationship is unlikely. Where such a request does occur, in my experience, the employee may be referred to an outside specialist or organization. Therefore, the chances of an internal trainer providing formal counselling is quite rare. My definition of formal counselling is as follows:

Formal counselling

- The counselling relationship embraces all the stages as described earlier in this chapter.
- It is a contractual relationship, i.e. the roles of counsellor and client are specified and agreed.
- The parties to that relationship agree in advance when, and for how long, they will meet.
- There will be an agreed meeting place, free from interruptions, for the sessions.

- Counselling will be recognized as a legitimate activity by the organization.
- Counselling will be seen as an activity that needs to be kept separate from appraisal and performance schemes and from grievance and disciplinary interviews.
- The person who offers the role of counsellor is judged by the organization to have the requisite skills and abilities to provide that service.

Ideally, not only should these criteria be met, but there should also be a clear statement to all employees about the nature of the service and how it can be accessed.

Informal counselling

What does happen in organizations, however, *irrespective of the official attitude*, is what I would describe as informal counselling. The distinguishing characteristics could include one or more of the following:

- It arises in the context of some other activity (e.g. during a training programme or consultancy activity; talking with an employee about training and development needs and activities etc.).
- It arises from an immediate crisis in the client's life.
- It is likely to be a unique experience, i.e. the first time that the person has taken up the role of client.
- The 'request' for counselling may not arise cleanly or clearly but emerge from an expressed desire to talk over a situation or as an attempt to clarify feedback.
- It is likely to be a one-off situation, i.e. the parties may never resume this kind of relationship.
- The client is distressed or troubled as a result of another learning experience.
- There are obvious limits of time and choice of environment for offering the counselling.

The distinction I have drawn between formal and informal has an importance over and above the simple differences in how counselling arises. *Trainers need to be aware that they must set some important limits when engaged in informal counselling.* The first limit is the need to acknowledge as soon as possible that a counselling relationship has developed or is in the process of developing. Such an acknowledgement provides a necessary safeguard for both parties to make a clear decision about whether they want this to happen and at this time. The second limit is the one imposed by the constraints of time. Whatever those constraints may be (say, 25 minutes) there is still a need to cover the stages of counselling, particularly that of managing the closure. The third limit is that of helping the client to manage the immediate crisis by identifying ways in which he or she can develop both internal and external support systems. An unhelpful choice under these circumstances is to encourage the client to explore other aspects of the problem or to go looking for 'the answer'. The fourth limit is always to be mindful of the fact that the client may be returning to an environment where he or she may not have access to other counselling resources. If the trainer is able and willing to offer further support then this does take pressure off the immediate situation. Similarly, if the trainer can offer details of specialist counsellors that the client can use in the future this is also helpful.

When informal counselling arises during a training programme the trainer may well have the opportunity to direct the need into some aspect of the formal programme. For example, when the programme contains workshop activity or back-home planning then the client can address their concerns into those contexts. It is worth being aware, however, that some course members make such requests of the trainer as a way of *avoiding* having to deal with issues that are really the property of the learning group. A simple example of this may be where one course member requests counselling from the trainer about dealing with another member of the group. To offer counselling under these circumstances is to not only collude with that individual but to collude with the process of avoidance in the group, i.e. the trainer ends up defusing conflict.

By contrast, those individuals who turn up on a programme having experienced the cycle of avoidance are often in desperate need of counselling. Despite their antagonism to the trainer and the programme (see p. 64) they are also looking for such help. Providing that the trainer is able to keep some relationship with them, particularly at the beginning of the programme when their criticisms and discontent are at their sharpest, then they are likely to make the request. Often just being willing to listen and accept their views is the first step into the counselling relationship.

Constraints on the internal counsellor

Even where the trainer can offer both formal and informal counselling he or she is likely to operate with constraints that would not apply to an external counsellor. Some of these constraints I have already mentioned: the attitude of the organization to counselling; demands which conflict with the trainer's freedom to offer counselling (i.e. when they are also involved in some appraisal of employees), in particular where these may conflict with a need for confidentiality.

Problems of confidentiality can also arise when clients offer information about their actions which are clearly illegal or unacceptable to the organization (e.g. stealing money or goods; falsifying records etc.). How the trainer chooses to respond under these circumstances may be clearly laid down by the organization, i.e. they must be reported. If the trainer is free to use discretion on how to respond then he or she needs to be clear about an appropriate course of action to use before such an eventuality does arise. Whatever that choice is the client needs to be told clearly at the time. My choice is to ask the client to make public that action and to offer whatever support may be required to enable him or her to cope with the situation.

The trainer's expertise and willingness to explore issues will also be a constraint. He or she might limit themselves to clearly contained 'work problems' and avoid dealing with domestic issues which intrude on the work situation. Even without this clear division there may be some specific issues (e.g. divorce, bereavement etc.) that they find difficult to deal with or they judge needs specialist support. In which case they may refer the client to outside expertise.

Whatever limits the trainer operates with the clients are also likely to set limits on the kinds of issues they wish to raise or the depths they are willing to explore. In which case the trainer can still offer a very useful service to the client and to offer referral as and when appropriate.

It seems possible, whatever the current constraints, that counselling can become an increasing and valuable part of the learning and development activities provided by organizations. One of the factors which will determine if, and how, this may occur, will be the attitude and practices of internal trainers. One of the worst dangers, in my view, will be if a significant number of trainers start to 'play' with counselling in the same way that an earlier generation dealt with therapy-based approaches to interpersonal skills training in the 1960s and 1970s. What is required instead is a responsible and integrated approach.

Summary

In this chapter I have looked at some of the current organizational attitudes to counselling, and how these are likely to affect the nature and quality of what trainers can provide. A six-stage model of counselling, based on the helping relationship, is then described and illustrated with examples drawn from organizational experience. This discussion of counselling provides an opportunity to examine the paradox of change which lies at the centre of all learning interventions. To illustrate this paradox I have drawn on the experiences of clients who have received effective counselling. An important distinction is then drawn between the two types of counselling—the formal and informal—that the trainer is likely to offer to learners. Finally, I have discussed some of the practical constraints in which the internal trainer has to work.

In the next chapter I will look at the helping relationship in consultancy.

References

1. British Association of Counselling, *Codes of Ethics and Practice* (BAC, 1987).
2. Brigid Proctor, *Counselling Shop* (Burnett Books, 1978).
3. Ian McMonagle, *Counselling for Work*, MA dissertation, Lancaster University (September 1988).

Informal counselling

This example of informal counselling benefits from the fact that I am able to use the recorded experiences of the client, Ian McMonagle, for illustration. The counselling took place in May 1988 and Ian's account was published in September of that year as part of his MA dissertation for Lancaster University.[1]

The background

In May 1988 Ian, who was at that time employed by HM Customs and Excise, and I were running a one-week residential programme for a group of twelve regional training officers of that organization. The programme was both complex and very demanding. For example, we had designed a conference structure for the fourth day of the programme which not only involved our providing a number of separate sessions during that day, but also meant introducing other trainers who were new to the group to provide specialist sessions.

When we were designing the programme (March) we agreed to devote some time each evening to reviewing the programme and offering each other feedback as appropriate. It was during the review on Thursday evening that the need for counselling was identified and acted upon.

The counselling

Ian's account of what happened is as follows:

I was aware of something which was 'niggling' within me. My route into identifying what it was centred upon my request for some feedback. My choice was a man for whom I had personal and professional respect. I had set an important ground rule, the individual from whom I wanted time, attention and respect was my choice, as was the timing of my approach and the place—a quite corner in a large room of a hotel which was open to the public. The process was very satisfying perhaps because I recognized the skills and qualities of the counsellor and felt safe as a consequence. I've produced a number of words to describe the situation and what it felt like [see Figure CS3.1], some of which are self explanatory, however some significant aspects were:

• The counsellor freely offered his experience of me over the previous week and on a moment by moment basis.

Process seemed
natural

Straight talking — absence of jargon
Total attention

Guessed that there was something in it
for counsellor — perhaps a feeling of
being valued

He offered time perspective

Future — past — present
Optional follow-up, my decision
'It's quite normal'
Willingness to share
'Soft' words used
No liberties being taken

Talked out of friendship

Trusted his motives
Counsellor knows how to have fun
In touch with himself

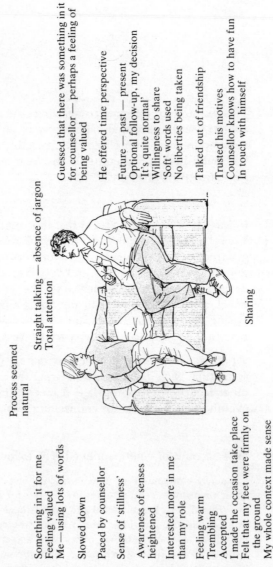

Something in it for me
Feeling valued
Me — using lots of words

Slowed down

Paced by counsellor

Sense of 'stillness'

Awareness of senses
heightened

Interested more in me
than my role

Feeling warm
Trembling
Accepted
I made the occasion take place
Felt that my feet were firmly on
the ground
My whole context made sense

Sharing

Safe
Not conspicuous

Background noise (buzz)
Worked with individual for short time

Retained my separateness but felt briefly joined in my situation. Felt as if hugged? Recognized a peer-level conversation was taking place. Absence of any upmanship/downmanship. Adult : adult relationship. Sense of being served. Genuineness — 'non-techniqued' — I'm not a 'number', not a 'case', not a problem — although I *had* a problem. Realization of genuine support from others I'd discounted. Focus turned outward, unburdened, relaxed, aware of my options, my choices, readiness to move on.

- The interest from the counsellor was in me primarily and then in my role(s).
- There was no 'taboo' content, I was able to talk about my faith without receiving uncomfortable signals from the counsellor.
- While I retained my separateness I felt briefly joined in my situation.
- The time perspective included past events, future anticipation and present reality.
- My senses were heightened in awareness.
- I was treated with kindness and respect, there was in no sense any one-upmanship, e.g. I'm OK—you're not OK.
- How I felt about my situation made a lot of sense.

The session lasted for about ninety minutes but we went through all the stages of counselling.

Comments

Although I have referred throughout the previous chapter to informal counselling only in the context of trainer and course member, this example does illustrate the incidence of trainer-to-trainer counselling. Not only does this type of counselling take place regularly, it is often formally agreed between co-trainers that they are willing to provide this service as a way of offering support to each other. These agreements recognize that in providing events for others, issues of personal learning are also likely to emerge for the trainer. Without such support in these circumstances the trainer can struggle to remain effective in helping others to learn and change.

Some important factors about this counselling experience were as follows.

1 Although this was the first time that we had co-trained, I had known Ian for six years and therefore had a lot of information about his capacity to learn and his ability to integrate new experiences. In my judgement this type of knowledge is far more important than that of biographical detail.
2 As professional trainers we were equally aware of what counselling involved and therefore managed the contractual issues effectively.
3 Because of the demands of the programme our tiredness was a useful deterrent to the ever-present dangers of attempting to cover too much ground or looking for the 'answer'.
4 Despite the environmental constraints (e.g. venue, tiredness etc.) both of us felt energized by the experience. Ian reports that, 'I felt very energized and optimistic, my attention and my senses were very sharp'. This kind of energy release is something that I experience as a trainer in many different learning contexts, and it is usually related to a clear decision, as on this occasion, not to work hard or push for learning. I, therefore, use my sense of tiredness as a barometer for effectiveness, i.e. if the level becomes oppressive it is a sign that I am taking too much responsibility for the learning of others.

Reference

1. Ian McMonagle, *Counselling for Work*, MA dissertation, Lancaster University (September 1988).

Formal counselling

Although specialist counselling organizations and therapists have developed their own patterns of counselling (usually in the context of a relationship that lasts for months or years) there is no clear pattern for a formal counselling relationship within organizations. Therefore, I, like other trainers, have developed a pattern that makes sense to me. This example illustrates the pattern that I have adopted.

The background

In early 1986 I was approached by the training officer of a company in the south-east of England to discuss the possibility of offering formal counselling to his managing director. Arising from their discussions they agreed, for slightly different reasons, that they did not want to use the services of either specialist counselling organizations or to approach therapists. Their objections to these potential sources were (1) to avoid a long-term relationship; (2) a discomfort about the connotations of therapy; and (3) a concern about stepping into unknown areas of expertise and approach. They were also concerned that the potential counsellor should have some organizational experience and knowledge. The trainer, who had attended courses that I provided, approached me to discuss the possibility of providing a service. On the basis of that discussion I then spoke to the client on the telephone and we made the appropriate agreements.

The counselling

On my suggestion we agreed to three counselling sessions of two hours each to be spread over a period of ten weeks. These sessions would take place off the company's premises. I also indicated that it was likely that I would ask the client to undertake tasks between sessions. As preparation for the first meeting I asked the client to make some notes on how he would like to be different in behavioural terms.

At the start of the first session we clarified roles and expectations. In terms of my role it was agreed that I would:

- Ask questions.
- Pay attention to both what he said and how he said it.

- Give him feedback about my observations of his behaviour, and my emotional responses.
- Help him to develop a greater awareness of self and how he was managing the situation.
- *Not* offer solutions or an answer.

Despite being taken aback by my request to define how he wanted to be different he had done the task which had helped him to redefine the nature of his concerns. I told him that my reason for making such a request was to make him more aware of how his behaviour was an important factor in the problem situation. Near the end of the session we were exploring how he habitually repressed certain of his feelings. The 'homework' that I set him for the next session was to make a written note of such occasions.

At the start of the second session I asked him if he detected any pattern linking these occasions. What emerged was a pattern of holding back on small resentments and disappointments and then exploding with anger. Near the end of the session we had moved on to explore one of his important relationships in which he found it difficult to express care and affection. The 'homework' I set him for the third session was to make a note when this had occurred, and in particular to pay attention to the ways in which he stopped himself from expressing such feelings (e.g. being fearful of being rejected).

The third and final session explored this area in great detail and then moved on to the client's summarizing what he had learnt from the counselling experience. We both agreed that this was a good time to close the relationship.

Comments

This was the client's first experience of counselling and, despite his obvious need for help, I was aware that he was tentative and uncertain about the prospect. Hence the objections to a specialist agency. My judgement was that he also needed a kind of road-map for the journey. This explains both my choice of the preparatory work and a listing of the behaviours that I would adopt as a counsellor.

Although the initial arena he provided for his problems was the work situation, what was really causing him most discomfort was a domestic relationship. The relationship, however, was influencing his work behaviour. This surfaced in the second session and was worked through by the middle of the last session.

I have used this format (an agreement to three sessions plus 'homework') on other occasions. My judgement, which I share with clients at the start, is that if they are not in a position to be managing themselves more effectively by that stage then (1) the counselling is ineffective, or (2) the client needs to use specialist resources and a long-term helping relationship.

5 The consultancy relationship

The word 'consultancy' is widely used in organizations to describe any activity carried out by a specialist who may, or may not, work full-time for that organization. The specialist knowledge or skills involved may be technological, e.g. computer applications; procedural, e.g. recruitment services; structural, e.g. designing organization structures or job-evaluation schemes. What unites this array of consultancy activities is a recognition by the organization that it needs to use the services of experts to deal with a specific problem. Organizations also use other types of consultants whose terms of reference and skills are less easily defined. Such experts would define themselves, though the organization may not think of them in such terms, as organization development consultants. Organization development (OD) has been defined by Richard I. Drake and Peter J. Smith[1] as:

a planned and integrated approach to change which considers the organisation as a whole.

The expertise of the OD consultant, which is often less immediately obvious than other specialists, consists of an understanding of *organizational processes*, i.e. how organizations work. Specifically, this knowledge should include both organization theory (how to organize to carry out tasks) and the behavioural sciences (how individuals and groups behave in organizations). The role of the OD consultant, in my opinion, is to bring that knowledge to the service of the organization with a view to developing not only a planned and integrated approach to change but also to develop *a process of learning which mutually includes both the consultant and the client or the client system*. It is this intention and methodology which actually distinguishes the OD consultant from other types of consultants who offer their services to organizations. It is the contention, that will be developed in this chapter, that the establishment of the consultancy relationship, based on the principles of the helping relationship (see p. 23 *et seq.*), is the major determinant of an effective OD change strategy.

For many trainers working in organizations the desire to move from the relatively simple role of running courses to that of providing a consultancy service, as described above, appears to involve a monumental leap of both role and expertise. As long as they appear to view it in these terms then the desire will remain unsatisfied. A more realistic approach would recognize that what is required is an incremental development both in expertise and role based on a greater willingness to step into uncertainty. What the trainer must be prepared to give up is the comfortable certainty of expertise that he or she has gained from being 'in charge' of a training event. Any trainer who has learned to develop a helping relationship in the training room already has the primary skills to provide a consultancy service in the organization.

The organizational perspective

Any trainer undertaking a consultancy activity needs to have a view of how organizations function. Whether that view is 'correct' or 'fashionable' is in my judgement less important than the fact that such a perspective is necessary before taking any steps as a consultant. Without a map it is difficult to undertake a journey. (For the trainer who is new to this area then *Writers on Organisations* by D.S. Pugh, D.J. Hickson and C.R. Hinings[2] provides a useful collection of maps.)

The organizational perspective that particularly informs my work as a consultant is that of systems theory. Apart from its own particular merits it shares a basic assumption with Gestalt therapy that the organism (in Gestalt, the person; in systems theory, the organization) is primarily concerned with its continuing relationship with the environment. In the same way that a person is dependent on manipulating the outside world to satisfy his or her whole range of physiological and psychological needs, the organization is continually having to adjust and respond to its environment. Failure to manage this relationship leads to the same consequences at both the personal and organizational levels (i.e. the organism's ability to survive is seriously impaired).

One of the key figures involved in applying systems theory within organizations was Eric Trist. Based on work undertaken while at the Tavistock Institute he developed the model of organizations as socio-technical systems.[3] In addition to viewing organizations as organisms being involved in managing and responding to their environment, he also saw organizations as being made up of separate but overlapping systems, each of which is engaged with managing its boundaries with other systems. In particular, he described an organization as comprising three distinct but highly interrelated sub-systems (see Figure 5.1).

Despite the fact that the sub-systems are described as discrete, a key concept of the model is that a change in one (e.g. the introduction of new technology) is likely to have major implications in the other two areas (e.g. structure, expertise *and* attitudes, behaviour etc.). What Trist discovered in his consultancy work was that, when organizations introduced specific changes, their planning and implementation of that change did not take sufficient account of its likely consequences in the other areas, *especially* the impact on the informal social system. One aspect of this failure is a view that still often pertains in organizations that employees will always resist change *whatever the intrinsic merits of the proposal.* People are labelled reactionary, deviant and obstructive, and their behaviour described as irrational and destructive. While recognizing that the common reaction to change is likely to embrace feelings of uncertainty and anxiety, the resultant behaviours are more to do with the way change has been managed than it has to do with human nature!

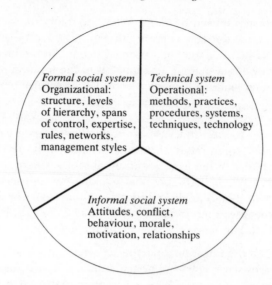

Figure 5.1 *The socio-technical system*

The need for consultancy

When senior managers become aware of problems within the organiz-ation they have a tendency to look for mechanistic solutions, particu-larly in the formal and technical systems, e.g. restructuring, introduction of new procedures etc., *or the identification of a training need*. The nature of these solutions often exacerbate the problem, particularly when as is often the case, the quality of analysis is poor. The problem that they are attempting to deal with usually manifests itself in some aspect of the informal social system, e.g. low morale, lack of cooperation, poor com-munication or a conflict between the formal communication system and a flourishing 'grapevine'. The solution—usually an attempt to change something or someone—simply imposes more uncertainty and pressure on a system which is already unable to cope with what is already hap-pening. It is at this stage that the senior manager is likely to turn to the internal trainer with a request that he or she provide a training pro-gramme on 'assertion', 'influencing skills', 'effective team work', or some equally suitable area of perceived deficiency. If the trainer has already established a relationship with the line manager then he or she may be called in for consultations before the problem has been packaged in this way. Regardless of when the trainer is approached, he or she has a clear choice on how to respond. The 'trainer's' response would be to meet the need as defined by the line manager; the 'consultant's' response would be to see the defined need as a starting-point.

Either of these responses would involve a consultancy service being offered to the client. The former would be similar to the other types of consultants used by organizations, i.e. a technical expert. The latter response would be that of an OD consultant, i.e. a process expert. The ability to respond in either of these ways—and the internal trainer will need that flexibility of action—is dependent on a number of factors. The principal factors are:

1 Client's expectations—what do they want from the situation? A quick fix, or a willingness to invest their time in dealing with the problem? Are clients willing to accept ownership of the problem, or do they see the problem as arising from the deficiencies of others?
2 The nature of the problem—does the defined need make sense? Does the target population actually need skills in assertion or effective teamwork? Can the prescribed training solution also be seen by clients as a method of analysis for identifying more fundamental problems?
3 Consultants' expertise and confidence—do they feel ready to enter into the uncertainty of an OD consultancy activity? Do consultants trust not only themselves but also their clients?
4 Do both parties have the necessary time and resources to undertake the project?

If on consideration of these factors the trainer chooses the latter response—to be an OD consultant—then the defined need becomes a starting-point for a cycle of activity which embraces the following stages:

- analysis
- diagnosis
- implementation
- review

The consultancy cycle

Although these are offered as sequential stages in the process of consultancy, most projects are unlikely to be so clearly defined. The project may actually start at the implementation stage. For example, my entry into a social services department was on the basis of being asked to review the effectiveness of briefing groups which had just been introduced; or see Case Study Five on running a team building event for a senior management team. Additionally, wherever the consultant starts, he or she will find that they have to move both up and down the different stages. Indeed, the review stage should ensure that further analysis, diagnosis, and implementation need to take place. For the sake of clarity, however, I shall discuss each of these stages in the above order.

Analysis

The objective of analysis is to discover how the system works, and involves: identifying types of information available (see page 86), collecting and structuring the information, and making decisions about the nature and quality of information.

Information collection

Hard information is often easy to collect and is already usually structured. It is factual and presents a picture of the organization in terms of what it *should be*.

Soft information requires intervention by the consultant and comes from discussion and observation. The extent to which the consultant wishes to impose structure (e.g. the use of questionnaires) or to allow structure to emerge (e.g. through interviews, and/or meetings) is a matter of choice. It is important to recognize, however, that during the act of

Information available

In the context of consultancy there are three types of information:

Hard information	*Soft information*
Organization structures	Opinions
Agendas	Perceptions
Minutes of meetings	Feelings
Recorded decisions	Behaviour
Procedures	Relationships
Systems	
Statistics	
Policy/marketing decisions	
Technical changes/decisions	

History
Whether written or verbal, likely to be a mixture of 'hard' and 'soft'.

---

collection the consultant is not only shaping the information (i.e. choosing what to collect), but is also influencing the system being analysed. For example, in the act of talking to people the consultant is likely to arouse a number of future expectations about consultation, feedback, or action which the organization may meet or disappoint. It may also lead members of staff to talk to each other about their discussions with the consultant (which in itself may be a new experience for that part of the organization). For these reasons, the consultant needs to be aware that he or she is already influencing the system being analysed. Therefore, the picture that is presented by this soft information can either be *what is* or *what was*. For example, having interviewed a team member about his or her perceptions of the team, and his or her contribution to meetings, it is not uncommon for that person to begin modifying their behaviour at future meetings—particularly if they know that they will be taking part in a team-building event.

The consultant brings to the analysis a wealth of experience, beliefs, interests, blindspots etc, which also affect not only the information that is selected but the way that information is likely to be structured. For instance, a consultant with a special interest in induction may not only pay particular interest to staff experiences in this area but may choose to see any problems there as being causative of wider problems in the organization, e.g. low morale.

Not least as a source of information is the consultant's reactions to people and events. How he or she is treated by people in the organization—welcomed, or treated with suspicion—is merely one source of information. Equally valid is the atmosphere or climate within the organization. Does it seem to be a safe place to make mistakes? Are individuals left to their own resources, or are they encouraged to ask for help? How open are people to each other? What does the consultant enjoy or find difficult about his or her working relationship with the department?

Making decisions

Given the plethora of information available, there is often a need to make decisions about the quality of information, i.e. what is important and what can be trusted.

If all the parties are agreed on the analysis then such decision-making is not required. However, when choices have to be made then the following guidelines are offered:

1 Soft information is generally more important than hard—it tells you what *is* rather than what *should be*.
2 Avoid looking for consensus with soft information. The diversity of feeling or opinion is in itself likely to be an important issue. For example, if one team member is very unhappy and the others differ only in terms of their degree of satisfaction then at least one problem is being ignored by the team.
3 Aim to involve the client and the client system in as much of the analysis as possible. Not only does this directly involve them in the learning process, it also serves to safeguard the blindspots of the consultant.
4 If there is any doubt, the consultant should honour and respect his or her perceptions and feelings. The reason for this is not to imply that the consultant is the best judge but as a discipline for bringing to the surface the subjectivity that would otherwise contaminate a false objectivity. For example, unless I am unable to acknowledge my distrust and/or dislike of a person I am likely to pay more attention to information that is critical of him or her and choose not to see those aspects that others appreciate.

Diagnosis The objective of diagnosis is to identify the real problem(s) as opposed to the 'felt' need (the same distinction as in counselling, see Chapter 4). This is not to imply that in any situation there is likely to be a single problem that is the start of a simple causative chain, e.g. poor communication procedures—lack of information—staff dissatisfaction—poor relationships—low productivity.

The real problem(s) are simply those conditions which have a major impact on a particular system and are experienced as important factors by a large number of the population. So to return to the above example, poor communication procedures may be a source of grievance for many people but may not be related to, or indeed account for, other conditions, e.g. dissatisfaction, staff turnover. Indeed, poor communication procedures may result from a different cause, e.g. inappropriate management style. One of the consequences of using systems theory as a diagnostic tool is to eschew the simple causative model illustrated above in favour of a more realistic, though more complex, framework which could be shown as in Figure 5.2.

The virtue of this kind of diagnostic framework is that it clearly shows the interrelatedness of all those factors and that in order to change the organization all aspects of the system need to be addressed. A particular path for intervention can be drawn from this framework (see Case Study Five where a similar diagnostic view informed my work with the London Borough of Hammersmith and Fulham), but clearly these factors could be recharted with a different factor replacing 'Inappropriate management style'. *As long as all the listed factors are addressed then any number of different implementation strategies could be used to equal effect.*

If, however, the implementation strategy is based on a linear causative

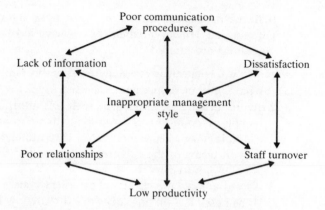

Figure 5.2 *Diagnostic framework*

model, i.e. poor communication procedures—lack of information—staff dissatisfaction—poor relationships—low productivity, then whatever is chosen is likely to be over-simplistic.

Because, in my judgement, the diagnostic stage is the most crucial part of an OD consultancy project, the client and the client system need to be heavily involved. Without such an involvement then (a) the consultant is excluding the client from the learning process; (b) the quality of diagnosis is impaired; and (c) the client is unlikely to have the necessary commitment to the implementation strategy.

In terms of moving from analysis to diagnosis, i.e. discovering the real problem(s), the following guidelines may be useful:

- The diagnosis is based on a consensual view of the client system (i.e. it is a majority view).
- There are obvious changes in the energy patterns of the client:
  —these changes may be positive (the eureka reaction);
  —these changes may be negative (hostility, avoidance and resistance).
- Growing interest and excitement at the prospect of change.
- The diagnosis makes sense.
- The consultant is asked to leave! (The prospect of 'real' change is too fearful).
- The system already shows signs of self-generated change.

In a system as complex as an organization, it is highly unlikely that there is a single major problem (a person, a procedure, a training need etc.). Irrespective of this, the client and the client system may exert pressure, subtle or blatant, on the consultant to emerge with a simplistic diagnosis. In most cases this kind of pressure is likely to represent an avoidance of responsibility by the client, or significant others in the organization, of their contribution to the problem. Even in extreme cases—a tyrannical boss for instance—the problem embraces not only the behaviour of the boss but also the behaviour of the subordinates. For whatever reason, they have colluded in developing and sustaining the problem. Such avoidance can be easily discovered in situations where members of a team will talk about a 'relationship problem' between two of their colleagues which affects the performance of the team. Implicit in such descriptions is an assumption that the problem is 'out there', and has nothing to do with the behaviour of the speaker. At a simple level, the reality is that all team members are contributing to that problem—even if it is only at the level of being willing to tolerate the existence of the problem. In addition, they might also be contributing their disapproval, denial, avoidance to one or both parties. Whatever the nature of their contribution they are allowing the conflict to become polarized between the two people concerned, thereby ensuring that it becomes impossible to resolve. In my experience, such 'personality clashes' are invariably based on a conflict involving the whole team, e.g. lack of trust or cooperation etc., in which the two protagonists 'act out' the drama on behalf of the team.

The consultant who approaches such problems on a simplistic basis, in this case attempting to repair a 'personality clash', is likely not only to exacerbate the immediate problem, but also to collude with the rest of the team in their avoidance of responsibility.

Implementation

Whatever the nature of the change strategy to be implemented there are some general guidelines that the consultant needs to consider. These are as follows.

- Commitment to the strategy has to be widely shared, i.e. wider than the client and the consultant. At the very least the senior management of the organization must be actively involved.
- This commitment is demonstrated by people exercising responsibility for different aspects or stages of the strategy.
- There is a clear need to recognize that implementation is not an end-state but a stage in the cycle. This means that monitoring may reveal the need for further analysis or diagnosis and/or modification of the change strategy.
- The key responsibility of the consultant at this stage is to plan for his/her exit from the client system. Having reached this stage in the process of change the consultant should have ensured that appropriate skills and understanding have been developed within the organization. Any consultancy activity which depends on the continuing presence of the consultant is doomed to fail.
- The main aim of OD consultancy is to develop a continuing learning system in the organization, so at this stage—if not before—it is important that formal learning reviews are introduced. Such learning reviews should include the client, the consultant, and the client system identifying what each has learned from the activity. The learning to be at two levels: one, about changing the organization; two, what each person has learned about him- or herself.
- The strategy must be capable of modification in the light of feedback and experience.
- However effective the consultancy it must always be borne in mind that even those individuals committed to the strategy will experience anxiety, uncertainty, and doubts. (This is also true for the consultant.) Anticipating these likely issues, and being prepared to deal with them

explicitly as they happen, will help to manage the process of change more effectively.

- The consultant needs to recognize his or her own needs for support and assistance. Not the least important type of support is that of personal feedback from the client and the client system. If such support is not readily forthcoming then a clear option is to ask for some! Additionally, the consultant also needs support from outside the organization, if only to provide a different perspective. (This central issue of support is something I want to address at more length in the next chapter.)

Finally, the consultant needs to ensure that the client system understands that change is a *process* and not an event. Change is occurring all the time in organizations: sometimes it is planned, but much of it stems from responses both inside and outside the organization, e.g. a new member joins the staff, central government raises interest rates etc. The organization needs to learn how to manage these changes, as well as any it chooses to introduce in a planned way. Their ability to do so depends on what they have learned about the process of learning and change.

Review Reviewing and learning from what happens during the project is only one aspect of what an effective review procedure should be concerned with. A wider and more fundamental purpose of review is to establish what I would call the *learning organization*, i.e. an organization which regularly and systematically analyses and evaluates both the *processes* and *structure* with which it operates. Such a task goes much wider than the normal procedure of comparing performance year on year. Simply to measure the organization in terms of balance-sheet performance, e.g. productivity and profitability, is to be essentially concerned with the short-term. The speed and pace of change facing all organizations in the UK has increased dramatically in the last thirty years and all the indicators would suggest that the future holds more of the same (e.g. the Single Market of 1992; the present government's 'restructuring' of public bodies to make them more self-sufficient and competitive in a market economy). The ability of all organizations to survive in this climate will be dependent on their capacity and willingness both to learn from and manage the process of change.

Irrespective of the particular change strategy that may be desired, the primary aim of the OD consultant is to develop *a process of learning which mutually includes both the consultant and the client or the client system* (see p. 84 *et seq*). In that respect the change strategy is merely the vehicle for ensuring that this occurs. At its simplest level this merely involves meeting regularly with the client to review what has happened, and what each has learnt from the experience. During the course of the project the aim of the consultant is to pass responsibility for these reviews to the client system. The success of achieving this goal is dependent on building the appropriate consultancy relationship with the client.

The consultancy cycle is summarized in Figure 5.3.

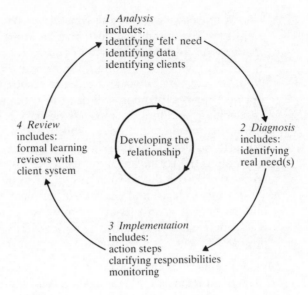

Figure 5.3 *The consultancy cycle*

The client relationship

Earlier in this chapter I stated that the crucial determinant of an effective change strategy is the nature of the relationship between the consultant and the client. Although it is my contention that the principles of the helping relationship (see p. 23 *et seq*) apply as much in this context as in those of training and counselling, it is important to recognize that, for a number of reasons, the consultant–client relationship is far more complex. Two immediate reasons for this complexity are: one, the focus for change is an organization rather than a training group or an individual; and, two, the consultancy relationship is usually of longer duration. (In some cases it can last for years.) Having acknowledged these two obvious factors, I would like to look in detail at some of the issues that give rise to the complexity.

The client

In the work of any consultant one of the most crucial issues is simply to determine who is the client. The invitation to the consultant may be from any number of sources, e.g. the training officer, the personnel specialist, head of department, or managing director. But the person who offers the invitation is not necessarily the client. The first question to face the consultant may be to determine who is the client for this project. Some important guidelines for identifying the appropriate person are:

- Who 'owns' the problem? (i.e. Who has identified the need and wishes to take action?) It might appear axiomatic that the most senior member of the organization should be the client, but unless he or she 'owns' the problem then the consultant would be wise to treat this person as a part of the client system, albeit a very important member. Ideally, the most senior member should occupy that role, and during the course of the project they may do so, but for the consultant to insist on that as a prerequisite is likely to be counter-productive.

- Who is most accessible to the consultant? At the early stages of any project the consultant will need regular access to a member of the organization for both information and to ensure that basic administration is provided, e.g. fixing up interview and meetings.
- Who can make decisions and provide resources? During the course of a project the organization will need to make a number of decisions, e.g. deciding on the next steps, taking part in the analysis, responding to information provided by the consultant, making people and rooms available, authorizing expenditure etc.
- To whom is the consultant accountable for his or her actions? In simple terms, the person the consultant reports to on progress.
- Who wants to learn and change? If the main contact or client views him- or herself as an agent of learning for others then the consultant would be well-advised either to find a different client or to leave the project.

My own preference for client in any project is to work with the top management team of the organization with the managing director or department head occupying the role of *primus inter pares*. In this situation the team would be my client and would fulfil the role described above, but I would be directly accountable to the leader and would see him or her as my primary client. The reasons for my preference are as follows.

1 The responsibilities of the client as described above are usually too demanding for one person to be able to meet in addition to carrying out their normal management duties.
2 To attempt any meaningful change in an organization without the top management team being an integral part of the process is to make the chance of success fairly slim.
3 The most effective way to change an organization, in my experience, is to focus on changing appropriate sub-systems like teams or groups, rather than individuals.

Irrespective of preferences the consultant can only start with the person offering the invitation and the proposed point of entry. From this starting point he or she can begin to express preferences. (In Case Studies Five, Six and Seven, all had very different entry points but each led to involving the senior management teams at some point in the activity.)

During the course of a project (Case Study Five is an example of this) the activity will involve the consultant in developing a relationship with a number of sub-clients (i.e. clients for particular aspects of the project), for example, working with individuals and groups at lower levels in the organization. Where this occurs the consultant needs to be clear, and make clear to all parties, the nature of the relationship between sub-clients and the client. In particular, there needs to be a clear understanding about what information is to be provided, where it goes, who receives feedback, and the levels of confidentiality that the consultant can offer. For example, when I begin discussing the prospect of team-building with members of a team the first item that needs to be cleared is to agree that all issues raised at that event are to be confidential, and that it is their collective responsibility if and how they choose to raise issues with senior management. In all respects, I seek to offer a helping relationship not only to the client but to every individual and group with whom I come into contact.

Consultancy roles

Having discussed some of the complexities of the client role it is appropriate to look at similar issues in respect of the role of the consultant. Having attempted to make a clear distinction at the start of this chapter between the role of the OD consultant and that of other consultants employed by organizations it is important to acknowledge some overlaps. In the pursuit of developing *a process of learning which mutually includes both the consultant and the client or the client system* the consultant may be required to provide different roles or styles. The nature of the project may dictate the need for a particular style, or the consultant may need to employ different roles during the course of one project. The most important factor which determines choice of role is how the organization initially defines the problem. In this respect it is possible to isolate and define at least three major roles.

Client-based

This usually starts from a position of the client saying something like, 'I've got a problem. I'm not sure how to define it, but I can describe what I am unhappy about. Can you help?' The features of this role are as follows.

- The client describes and owns the problem.
- The client takes responsibility for the strategy.
- The client is part of the client system and is open to learn.
- Responsibilities are shared and changing between the client and the consultant.
- The consultant works primarily with process (how the system works), rather than with the content (what does the system do).
- The consultant's dominant style is facilitator.
- The activities are more likely to be organic and less structured.
- Includes all four stages of the consultancy cycle, and starts with analysis.

(See Case Study Five.)

Problem-based

- The client defines the problem and sets parameters.
- The strategy is developed by the client and the consultant.
- The learning is aimed at a specific population.
- Responsibilities of the client and consultant are mutually defined at an early stage.
- The consultant works equally with process and content.
- The consultant's dominant style is that of trainer.
- The activities are more likely to be semi- or fully-structured.
- The project starts at the diagnostic stage of the consultancy cycle.

(See Case Study Six.)

Activity-based

- Both the problem and a strategy have been defined by the client.
- The learning is aimed at a specific population.

- The consultant is responsible for the activity but is likely to be directed by the client.
- The consultant works primarily with content.
- The consultant's dominant style is that of trainer.
- The activities are more likely to be structured.
- The project starts at the implementation stage of the consultancy cycle.

(See Case Study Seven.)

At first glance both the problem- and activity-based roles may appear to be examples of normal rather than OD consultancy, but, bearing in mind that these represent starting points only, it becomes clear that an effective consultant will need to work with this degree of flexibility. It is this flexibility which goes some way to meeting a concern often expressed by many internal trainers, and this is, 'How do I develop a consultant–client relationship?'

Developing the relationship

In all respects the relationship with a prospective client is no different from that with a course member or someone who seeks counselling. All three parties have the same concerns and make the same kinds of judgements about the trainer. These concerns are:

- 'Who is this person?'
- 'What can he or she do?'
- 'Can I trust him or her?'
- 'Will he or she help me?'

My own belief is that the particular concern internal trainers express about becoming consultants is sharpened by the fact that (a) clients are invariably senior to them in the hierarchy; and (b) they have to give up the certainty of their classroom expertise to take on this role. Both of these factors do bring to the surface doubts about confidence and competence. Instead of accepting these doubts as being self-generated many internal trainers project them on to the client, e.g. 'The client does not see me as being credible. How can I establish credibility?' Attempting to resolve the doubts by establishing credibility with the client can never be successful because not only is the effort addressed to the wrong person but it also serves to put the consultant in a one-down position. If the consultant is willing to use his or her doubts in a positive way, e.g. to take time, gain information, pay attention to the needs of the client etc., then he or she is taking better care of both parties.

From the point of first contact the consultant needs to invest time in getting to know the client at both a personal and professional level. The real concerns, listed above, that the client brings to the start of the relationship should be those that the consultant is also concerned about. In some instances the issues may have to be dealt with directly, e.g. 'It sounds like you don't trust me' *or* 'I would like you to offer me feedback'. As a general guideline, if the consultant has any doubts about what is happening in the relationship he or she should raise them as soon as possible. My preference, at the earliest opportunity (i.e. the first meeting) is to offer feedback to the client about my experience of him or her. This serves two purposes: one, it provides an important indication of how the client copes with feedback; and, two, it demonstrates a clear need I have to develop an open relationship with the client. For the same reason I also make a direct request for feedback, and agree with the client that if either of us are dissatisfied with what is happening then we state our concerns as they occur. My experience of most senior managers is that they respond very positively to this openness, not least because many of them are starved of feedback.

Unless these basic ground rules for the relationship are established early on, then when problems do occur—as they are bound to in the life of the project—they are harder to deal with. As the relationship develops then the issue of dependency will emerge. The client will begin to rely on the skills and knowledge of the consultant and choose not to value their own abilities. When this begins to occur the consultant will not only need to confront the behaviour of the client but will also need to examine what he or she may be doing to encourage the dependency, e.g. taking too much responsibility, appearing to be invulnerable to doubt or uncertainty.

Dependency affects both parties, and whatever the pay-offs in terms of, say, self-esteem, pride or needing to be wanted, the consultant who allows this to develop unchecked will pay a price, e.g. exhaustion, isolation, pressure etc. When dependency is not being managed effectively it is advisable for consultants to examine ways in which they are dependent upon clients i.e. what needs are they trying to satisfy in this relationship which should be met from other sources?

As a safeguard against the problem of dependency the consultant needs to plan to leave the client system at the earliest opportunity. It can be difficult to know when is the right time to leave, but, on balance, it is better to risk the danger of being premature in this respect. During the course of any project I begin consciously to limit my involvement from the stage of diagnosis and offer the client a date for my departure. Having agreed this time of closure enables both myself and the client to manage both the project and our relationship more effectively.

Summary

In this chapter I have looked at the range of activities that organizations would define as consultancy. I then discuss some of the problems that face the internal trainer who wants to develop a consultancy role in the organization. The opportunities for developing the role are outlined, and a practical model—the consultancy cycle—is then described. It is then argued that effective consultancy is dependent on developing a helping relationship with both the client and client-groups. Some of the key steps in building this relationship are then discussed, and a distinction is drawn between three different types of consultancy activity that the trainer can provide.

Having looked at the three major activities of training, counselling, and consultancy, in the final chapter I want to consider some of the important issues that affect the trainer.

References

1. Richard I. Drake and Peter J. Smith, *Behavioural Science in Industry* (McGraw-Hill, 1973).
2. D.S. Pugh, D.J. Hickson and C.R. Hinings, *Writers on Organisations*, 3rd edn (Penguin Books, 1983).
3. E.L. Trist 'The socio-technical perspective', in A. van de Ven *and* W.F. Joyce (eds), *Perspectives on Organisation Design and Behaviour* (Wiley-Interscience, 1981).

London Borough of Hammersmith and Fulham: Housing Department

The following is an example of what I have described as a client-based approach to consultancy (see p. 93 *et seq*). The project was started in February 1988 and my involvement ended in July 1989.

The context In the last ten years, particularly, local authorities have been subjected to a variety of pressures—economic constraints, changes in legislation, social and demographic changes, the impact of new technology, and not least, a central-government insistence on the development of an entre-preneurial approach to the provision of public services (e.g. privatization, competitive tendering). These pressures have impacted acutely on local-authority housing departments. In a recent compre-hensive review Professor John Stewart (Institute of Local Government Studies) has predicted that:

A local authority could lose large parts—or in theory all—of its stock through the combined effect of the right-to-buy, housing action trusts and tenant's choice.[1]

The very survival of housing departments, Professor Steward continues, will be largely dependent on their ability to develop 'a new management culture' to cope with this challenge. The nature of the required culture is one:

that gives meaning to the new roles of the housing departments, gives those who work within it a sense of purpose and fosters good relationships between those who carry out the many differing tasks involved. Organisational culture is the expression of the values that guides everything the department does. It is management's job to create, express and sustain the appropriate values.[2]

The Housing Department of the London Borough of Hammersmith and Fulham has an establishment of 650 posts. Like similar organizations it has a multi-levelled hierarchical structure in which decision-making is at some distance from the point of direct service to the public. At the start of the change strategy the members of the departmental management team described the prevailing culture of the organization as one characterized by:

- an overwhelming concern to complete tasks (with little concern for the values of these tasks to the quality of the services provided);
- being reactive rather than proactive;
- having little or no concern for the needs of employees;
- decision-making based on bewildering shifts between management autocracy or abdication;
- poor communication both up and down the structure;
- low morale and confidence among all staff;
- avoidance of personal responsibility for taking action;
- lack of trust and cooperation;
- a debilitating fear of making mistakes because of the perceived risks (real and imagined) of being punished for so doing.

In terms of rounding-out this portrait two important factors, not mentioned by them, but very apparent to an outsider, need to be included. One, in spite of these deficiencies, the level of personal commitment to providing a quality service to the public was (and still is) demonstrably evident among the vast majority of staff. Two, this honest self-appraisal could, with minor adjustments, be applied to other housing departments in England. What was particularly significant about the department was the willingness to take positive action rather than the nature or scale of the perceived deficiencies.

First contact

The request for me to work with the department was offered at short notice (some four weeks before a projected event) and in unusual fashion. The invitation actually came from the Local Government Training Board (LGTB) who were working with the department on developing a customer skills initiative called public-service orientation. One aspect of this initiative was for the departmental management team to undertake a team building event which the Local Government Training Board would finance and that I would run on their behalf. Three weeks before this event I attended a briefing at the Local Government Training Board given by one of their advisors and the policy and staffing officer of the department who was not a member of the management team. I was told at this meeting that the departmental management team (DMT) had readily agreed to the suggestion for the event; could only find two available dates (14 and 17 March 1988); and clearly wished to be an effective team before the arrival of the new director in April. (At this time a second-tier officer was acting-director and other members of the team were in acting-up posts.) I was also told that the DMT (seven members) had experienced a traumatic history. One symptom of their current malaise was that on agreeing to team-building the names of two consultants were advocated by members of the team, and because no agreement could be reached they decided to accept the impartial nominee of the LGTB. I, in effect, was the compromise consultant.

Having accepted this unusual invitation my first meeting with any (and all) of the team took place at the start of the team-building event. We started at 10.00 a.m. and finished at 6.15 p.m. As a consultant the only logical approach was to treat the two days as a diagnostic activity and to evolve a structure which reflected their agenda. What emerged was as follows:

Monday 14 March   10.00   Introductions
(Including: names; details about jobs; previous management training experience; expectations of the two days; expectations of each other; statement about how they were feeling at time)

10.45   Agenda setting
(Based on asking each person to identify their concerns about the team and about their membership of the team)

11.30   Unfinished business
(First priority they identified was their bad feelings about an ex-member of the team who had been, and still was, a powerful influence on their present behaviour with each other. I invited each of them to imagine that this person was sitting in an empty chair and to take the opportunity to express to him all the things they wished they had said)

2.00–   Unfinished business with each other
6.15   (Having 'cooperatively' dealt with a ghost they were ready to deal with each other. For this purpose I used a role negotiation exercise, with each person in turn offering feedback to colleagues on the basis of:

> I want you to do more of . . .
> I want you to do less of . . .
> I want you to continue doing . . .)

Thursday 17 March   10.00–   Unfinished business with each other
1.00   (Completing the activity from Monday)
2.00   Forward planning
5.00–   (In addition to agreeing action plans arising from the previous activity they tackled three priority areas:

> Time management
> Welcoming the new director
> Public-service orientation)

In the light of all the constraints (split days, no previous contact between consultant and team) it was extraordinary to experience their willingness and eagerness to engage in high-risk activities (e.g. a role negotiation exercise), and to see them begin to develop high levels of trust, support and cooperation with each other. It was clear to me that whatever their history of problems they were all committed to changing themselves and the department.

The acting director, David Beer, published his assessment of these two days in September 1988.

Neil has given us the principal tool with which to build our team (nobody else can build it for us). That tool is called 'process' and involves dialogue that not only addresses the task, but also the hidden agendas often linked to feelings and emotions that, if not openly discussed, hinder progress. In effect, 'process' is an agreement between the team to declare those hidden blockages . . . Experience has since proved that this is a difficult, but not impossible task and it gets easier the more you do it.[3]

The change strategy

At the end of that programme my relationship with the department was concluded, and, apart from reporting back to my client, the LGTB, I assumed that this would prove to be a limited intervention. Then I received an invitation to attend a meeting of the DMT, led by the new Director, John Newbury, on 17 May. At this meeting they agreed that team-building should be the principal vehicle for changing the culture of the organization. They believed that an awareness of, and skills in, process would be the means for changing both attitudes and behaviour within the department. I therefore agreed to provide:

1 A three-day residential team-building event for the DMT.
2 Six non-residential two-day team-building events for the divisional management teams.
3 Periodic reviews with the DMT about the progress of the strategy.

It was also agreed that the DMT would issue a document to all the managers who would be involved in team-building. This document would cover background information, aims of the programme, dates, and professional details about the consultant. In this document the aim of the strategy was described as follows:

The reason for taking this initiative is a concern to review past experiences and to develop a style of management which gives as much recognition to the needs of the people in the department as it has, in the past, to the needs to achieve the tasks of providing a housing service.

The staff were also informed that before each divisional team-building event (each of these teams were chaired by a member of DMT) they would have a chance to meet with the consultant and that the content of each two-day event would be determined by their own needs and interests.

The divisional teams

The first divisional team-building took place in July 1988 and the last was completed in February 1989. In all, ten teams have taken part. Two further teams were given the opportunity but at the pre-meeting decided not to go ahead. It had been agreed at the meeting in May that if teams or individuals did not want to take part—*for whatever reason*—then they could refuse. Three team members publicly chose not to attend their respective events and seven others were unable to because of sickness or other commitments. These exclusions obviously create problems (e.g. how to integrate the individual after) but I believe that more serious problems would have occurred if attendance had been made compulsory. Apart from the ethical concerns of forcing someone to attend a process event, that individual is likely to become the focus of attention to the detriment of problems more amenable to solution. Not least, there is an absurd paradox involved in coercing people to be more open and participative.

The common design for each event was based on a structure comprising four elements: introductory activities, role negotiation exercise, theory and action planning. The detail of the first element was as follows:

1 A brief outline of the four elements with rough guides on the likely timings of each element.
2 Personal introductions requiring everyone to state their name, any thoughts about the programme since the pre-meeting, and a statement about their feelings now.
3 Setting ground rules for the two days on:
   (a) my role (to provide guidance, structure and theory; to comment on how they talked to each other rather than on the content of what was said: to give feedback);
   (b) feedback (what it is—its purpose—and how to give and receive).
4 A theory input on the distinction between content and process in communications.

The second element, role negotiation, they had been asked to prepare for at the pre-meeting. This structured format for giving and receiving feedback enabled me to exercise the role of facilitator more clearly and cleanly for both the giver and receiver of feedback. It also provided the control to raise and deal with one issue, or relationship, at a time.

The third element, theory input on teams and group dynamics, reflects an ethical concern I have about process-based events. This concern is that people learn most effectively when they have some cognitive maps as well as experience.

The final element, action planning, took place at two levels: the individual and the team. Arising from feedback received, individuals made notes about their proposed changes of behaviour. This information was collated and circulated to all members after the event. The second level—team decisions—was agreed and listed on flipchart paper at the end of the second day. These agreements were of two kinds:

1 *procedural*   changes in membership, nature and circulation of agendas, frequency of meetings, the role of the chairperson etc.;
2 *process*   the adoption of ground rules for future meetings, e.g. the explicit giving and receiving of support, having regular process reviews as a team etc.

The nature of the action planning often took the form of contractual agreements between two or more individuals, e.g. 'I agree to give you feedback on monopolizing the conversation if you give me feedback on being too aggressive.'

The character of each event was remarkably different but all contained one critical incident, often near the end of the first day, which led to the disclosure and resolution of the major concern in the life of that team. This critical incident may have been an aggrieved subordinate criticizing a senior manager, or a problem relationship which had been affecting the whole team but which had been avoided or suppressed by all. These critical incidents were often highly emotional but without exception were skilfully managed by each team.

However, I am clear that some individuals did leave events with some unresolved issues, usually about themselves. Their ways of dealing with this varied. A couple took up my offer to contact me after; some worked it through for themselves; some talked through the issue with other members of the team at a later date. Two individuals managed their discomfort by being critical of the event afterwards, and actively sought out members of other teams due to attend later events to tell them what 'really happens' on team-building. The effect of these comments grew more sinister in the retelling and proved to be a decisive influence on the two teams who declined to take part.

One of the conclusions that I draw from this experience is that any attempt to change the culture of an organization—however efficacious in intent and implementation—will also have the effect of mobilizing resistance. For some individuals the prospect of change is so deeply threatening that they choose either to leave the organization or to escalate their resistance until they become totally isolated. This can mean that in the short term some aspects of organizational life can take a turn for the worse, e.g. higher staff turnover, increased uncertainty and anxiety, lowering of morale, exaggerated and unhealthy conflicts between individuals and groups. My own view is that this type of 'deviant' response has analogies with the process of adolescence. If, as Hammersmith and Fulham are attempting to achieve, the goal is to move away from a childlike-dependency culture then the first step (as in personal development) is to move into a period of adolescence which, for some individuals, can involve elements of rebellion and/or nihilistic despair. In the same way that we do not expect individuals to move from childhood to adulthood in an untroubled fashion, it is unrealistic to expect an organization to make such a transition in a short period of time. What the organization needs to do at this time is to find as many ways as possible to provide support to individuals and groups, e.g. clearer guidance to all on what is happening, ruthlessly effective communication channels, training, counselling, and a clear legitimization of the need to ask for and give support as a desirable characteristic of the effective manager.

The departmental management team

The second team-building event for the DMT was a three-day residential programme which took place on 21–23 September 1988. By the time this occurred, out of the original team of seven, one had resigned, and three new members had joined, including the director, John Newbury.

Apart from the obvious need to integrate the new team members and to build on the foundations of the first event, time was spent on planning and coordinating the wider project. From this time onwards, I became aware that the DMT, as a team and as individuals, began to exercise a healthy responsibility for the direction and control of the change strategy. There developed a more equitable balance in the client–consultant relationship. In subsequent meetings with them—for the agreed periodic reviews—they demonstrated a sense of collective purpose that had been absent in March.

At one such meeting in January 1989 a number of important decisions were made—not least to issue a 'position statement' to all members of the department about the immediate objectives of the DMT. It was also proposed that a 'facilitators group' be established in the department whose primary role was to replace the external consultant on completion of the team-building programme.

The facilitators group

From the start of the project I had been anxious to ensure that the continuation of the work did not become dependent on me as a consultant. As one of the aims of the project was to 'empower' managers to take a more proactive role in changing the organization, the logical development of that strategy was to establish an expertise to replace my own. It was decided to limit this group to ten people but to ensure that membership was open to all levels of the department. Accordingly, an open selection procedure for membership was undertaken by the department in April and May 1989. My role in this process was to brief all the prospective members and then to talk to the individuals about the technical aspects of facilitation.

In July 1989 I ran a five-day residential programme for the group. Of the ten members, eight had taken part in one or more of the team-building events that I had provided. Apart from that common experience, the group is drawn from different levels and divisions within the department.

The major feature of the programme that I designed for them was to provide each member with an opportunity to facilitate a group learning activity. Although some individuals had some previous experience of facilitating, the majority were approaching this activity for the first time. I also provided them with theoretical inputs on facilitation, intervention styles, learning theory (Gestalt psychology), and managing change in individuals and groups (Gestalt therapy). What became apparent during this programme was less their lack of experience but more their skills and abilities in facilitation. Having, over the years, provided many similar programmes for 'professional' trainers I was made acutely aware that whatever merits our professional expertise provides it can also be a massive handicap in providing learning experiences for others.

The facilitators group, which has been officially 'tasked' by the department began to operate in September 1989. The two objectives of the group are:

1 To act as a resource to all teams, groups or individuals in the department who request their service.
2 To take responsibility for raising process issues with any, and all, teams within the department. Such issues, of necessity, include the interface between the department and other parts of the local authority and the community it serves.

How the project continues and develops is now very much in the hands of the DMT and the facilitators group. My role, as external consultant, has been deliberately marginalized to that of being a resource to the facilitators group. They will decide on the nature of my future involvement.

Comments

The client   During the project the person of my client changed several times—the LGTB, the acting director, the DMT, the director, and the facilitators group. From May 1988 I was directly accountable to the director but my client, *in a learning capacity*, switched from that of the DMT to the facilitators group.

Empowerment   The primary aim of the project was to empower a dissatisfied and uncooperative management system with a view to move from a historical position of reactivity to one of taking responsibility for effectively managing change. That most of the managers were able to demonstrate, and quickly, that collectively and individually they possessed the skills to move forward is for me one of the most exciting discoveries of the project. The problem was not a lack of skill or understanding but a crucial lack of confidence and support.

Educational process   More than any other change strategy I have been involved with this one demonstrates to me that any attempt to change the culture of an organization is of necessity a long-term educational process. Even where people are heavily dissatisfied the prospect of change—no matter how participative or well-intentioned—can lead to entrenched resistance. Unless the nature of resistance is understood (see Chapter 2) it can never be properly managed. It is too easy for organizations to dismiss resistance as 'deviant' or to view it as an aspect of human nature which needs to be subverted or coerced.

The role of the consultant   Whatever the changes that have taken place in the department I am also aware of what I have learned from this project. First, and this was a major interest for me at the start, was to manage the issue of consultant–client dependency more effectively. The first step in this process was to recognize that dependency is a two-way process, i.e. not only can the client be dependent on the expertise of the consultant but also that the consultant can become dependent on the client (not least for financial reasons). In terms of managing my exit from the department I have erred, if at all, on the side of being too early. If so, I think this is infinitely preferable to the alternative.

Second, as a white middle-aged male, albeit with all the right liberal responses, I have discovered that my sensitivity to the views and needs of women, ethnic groups, the disabled etc. does not enable me to truly understand the differences in our experiences of the same, or similar, events. The organizational culture that exists, and will develop, at Hammersmith and Fulham holds the exciting possibility of more clearly and sensitively reflecting the needs and views of all the staff, not just those of the traditional power elite (i.e. white, middle-aged men). Such a change will also enable the organization to serve with greater sensitivity the needs of the community.

References

1. Professor John Stewart, *A New Management for Housing Departments* (Local Government Training Board, 1987), p. 13.
2. Ibid., p. 29.
3. David Beer and Veronica Coatham, 'Team building' in *Local Government Training Board Newsletter* (September/October 1988), 5.

Newcastle City Council: Architect's Department

The following is an example of what I have described as a problem-based approach to consultancy (see p. 93 *et seq*.). The project was started in November 1988 and my involvement ended in March 1989.

First contact

Prior to first contact with the client I had worked with the training officer of the local authority on providing two training programmes for representatives from all departments. These programmes were: 'Managing people' and 'Facilitator skills'. Apart from providing an opportunity to co-train with the internal trainer, these experiences also offered some understanding of the prevailing culture of the organization. (In all respects the similarities with the London Borough of Hammersmith and Fulham were striking, see Case Study Five.)

The client, the assistant city architect of the Architect's Department, had approached the training officer in September 1988 to talk about the possibility of some training intervention in the department. The training officer had then spoken to various members of the departmental management team to gain their perceptions. After these interviews the training officer approached me and we had a meeting with the client in November.

At this meeting the objective was clearly defined as the need for multi-disciplinary design teams to work more effectively together. Each of these teams is established in response to a particular project, and they have responsibility from the first contact with a client (e.g. the housing department) to final completion. The life of a particular project will vary from a few months to two years. Each team is led by an architect but during the project other disciplines (e.g. quantity surveying, engineering, etc.) are crucially involved at appropriate stages. Apart from the obvious problems of coordination and sequencing, the effectiveness of such teams is largely determined by the working relationships of the different disciplines. According to the client, the failure of the latter was responsible for problems with the former. Having raised the problem with his own management team, the assistant city architect had achieved agreement about exploring a training solution. Because of work pressures facing the department they were limited to a two-day training event for up to twenty people. At this meeting it was agreed that the training officer and I would attend a departmental management team in December (the senior representatives of each of the disciplines are members of the team) to (1) gain their views and (2) offer some proposals. It was also agreed that the event would take place in March 1989 at the Training Centre of Newcastle City Council.

The change strategy

Within the constraints imposed by the client—only two days and a group of twenty from the target population—the idea of a training programme on 'effective working teams' was obviously inappropriate. The immediate concerns of myself and the training officer were twofold: one, to focus on the practical problems that members of the teams experienced (i.e. to deal with the 'real' issues); two, to involve the departmental management team in the learning process and to gain commitment to future action in the department. So far we had only heard the views of the managers and could only guess at how far the design teams would experience the managers as part of the problem.

In designing the event we were particularly concerned about a number of issues: (1) the need to provide sufficient safety to enable a large group both to raise and take responsibility for the problems they were experiencing; (2) the need to tackle the problem of different professions working together; and (3) to involve the departmental management team directly in both the diagnosis and the identification of the change strategy. This last issue was particularly important—not least because we were unsure whether the group of twenty would share the perception of their managers that the design teams were experiencing problems! As it transpired our only contact with this group before the event was a document that the training officer sent to each member.

This document—headed, 'Working Better Together on Design Teams'—covered the background:

You will be aware of the financial and other pressures the Department faces as a result of competitive tendering, the need for greater quality assurance and other developments. To meet these challenges all the professions in the Department will need to work more closely together.

As a result of discussions of these needs with members of the Departmental Management Team, we have agreed to design a two-day workshop to tackle the issues involved in working together on design teams. This workshop will provide an opportunity for members of design teams to do some 'stock-taking', looking at the key issues lying around and then drawing up 'contracts' to deal with these issues. . .

And it also attempted to alert them to the first of the above concerns, i.e. safety:

To make the workshop effective we feel that all of us need to agree some clear ground rules on how we are going to work together on the real issues you face and ask you to adhere to them. We would like you to think about what ground rules you would need so you can feel comfortable openly discussing the issues that inevitably arise between members of design teams. We will agree on ground rules at the start of the workshop, so bring your list with you.

The event took place on 13–14 March 1989 and the group comprised five disciplines: architects, quantity surveyors, services engineers, structural engineers, and landscape architects. The structure of the workshop was as follows:

Monday	9.00	Introductions Aims of the workshop Ground rules
	9.45	*Effective teams* (Theory input on task, group and individual needs and on problems faced by groups)
	10.15	*Diagnostic exercise* (Small group exercise on diagnosing problems in design teams)
	11.00	Coffee
	11.15	Presentation of the above to the large group
	12.00	*Professional Goals* (Theory input on professional values, objectives and criteria: small group exercise based on professional groups)
	12.45	Lunch
	1.45	*Inter-disciplinary teams* (Each professional group was asked to prepare on flipcharts their answers to the following questions:
		How we see ourselves. . . How we see the other groups. . . How other groups see us. . .)
	2.45	Presentations of the above to the large group
	4.00	Tea
	4.45	Review of the day
	5.15	Close
Tuesday	9.00	*Team contracts* (Professional groups asked to prepare contracts of agreement for negotiation with the other groups)
	10.00	*Negotiations* (Of the above contracts)
	11.15	*Content and process* (Theory input and small-group exercise on problems of face-to-face communication)
	12.45	Lunch
	1.45	*Presentation of report to departmental management team* (The group were asked to prepare a presentation based on:
		Agreements reached between the professional groups Agreements required from departmental management team Agreements desired about the client relationship within the authority)
	3.15	Tea

3.30 *Presentation to the departmental management team*
(The client and two other members of the team listened to and offered an initial response to the report)
4.45 Review of the workshop
5.15 Close

Comments

The report was subsequently presented to the whole of the departmental management team and a detailed report of their response was sent to every member of the group on 26 April 1989. This report was written by the client, and addressed itself to eight of the issues that had been raised. In addition to responding to these issues it also included some additional proposals to assist design teams. This was then followed by a meeting between the client and all members of the group.

Although my involvement with the project ended in March 1989 the training officer of the authority has offered continuity, and some months after we meet with the client to review developments.

At the heart of the workshop was a standard inter-group exercise (i.e. how we see ourselves, how we see the others, how others see us) which I have used on similar events. Like any inter-group activity this can take a lot of time to work through to a satisfactory conclusion. It was particularly beneficial in this instance to undertake this activity with the training officer of the authority. Apart from the fact that he was able to provide a perspective of the organization that I would otherwise have had to spend some time developing, he is also able to provide both continuity and follow-up services for this particular project.

Sherratt & Hughes

The following is an example of what I have described as an activity-based approach to consultancy (see p. 93 *et seq*.). The project was started in October 1988 and my involvement ended in February 1989.

First contact Sherratt & Hughes, an enterprise of W H Smith Ltd, is a group of over fifty city and university bookshops in Great Britain and Europe. The group was formed in June 1986 with the objective of becoming the leading specialist booksellers in the country and the leading international English-language booksellers in Europe. (In the summer of 1989 Sherratt & Hughes would merge with Waterstones to form Sherratt & Hughes/Waterstones.)

About one year before this particular project I had been asked to design and provide a distance-learning programme for Sherratt & Hughes called 'First service'. The aim of this project was to promote the concept of service as being wider than the basic responsibility of serving the customer on the shop floor. The introduction to 'First service' offered a wider definition:

We believe that all members of the organisation are interdependent, they depend on one another. In fact, they are each other's customers.

This programme was undertaken by every member of staff and now forms part of the induction programme. From the start of this project Sherratt & Hughes had decided that a further training initiative would be required. To this end I attended the annual conference in September 1988 to discuss with, and receive feedback from, staff who had been involved in implementing 'First service'. The following month I was briefed by the operations director and the training officer on what was required as a second initiative. The area of training need was identified as that of selling skills, and, like 'First service', it was intended that all members of staff should undertake the programme. The brief was very specific in terms of content to be covered, and included:

- face-to-face selling skills
- product knowledge
- bibliographical skills

- developing confidence in salespeople
- an awareness of general promotion and image
- an awareness of services provided by the group
- an awareness of competitors
- customer knowledge

Unlike 'First service' I was given freedom to consider the best method for delivering the training but was told (1) training sessions would need to be constrained to the one-hour per week already allocated in shops, and (2) that if managers were to be used as trainers they would need appropriate training and documentation to run sessions.

Two other important factors, already known to me, needed to be taken into account. First, that the basic educational level of staff was generally higher than other retail establishments (some of the language of 'First service' had been experienced by some members of staff as patronizing). Second, that because of the essential tradition of 'browsing' in bookshops there was an obvious need to avoid any suggestion of attempting to introduce 'hard-selling' techniques.

The change strategy

Although the brief was very detailed there was a need for me to collect some additional information. This research involved (1) attending a meeting with senior managers at group office, (2) interviewing members of staff in a regional bookshop, and (3) spending a day in another bookshop simply listening to and observing interactions between staff and customers.

Based on this research I decided that the intervention, 'Active selling', should be a learning programme containing three parts:

Part 1—face-to-face skills
Part 2—the problem customer
Part 3—selling a service

The programme was designed to be implemented during training hours over consecutive weeks. As part of their detailed briefing managers were given freedom to arrange the time as they thought appropriate, and also to adapt the material for their own groups.

The programme

The programme was designed to be undertaken by groups of staff in each store with the branch manager taking the role of facilitator. (For more detail, see below.) The introduction to 'Active selling' sought to allay fears about what was on offer in the programme:

For many people the concept of 'selling' and 'selling skills' is likely to have connotations of manipulation, deviousness and dishonesty. The assumption being that the 'art' or 'science' of selling is based on persuading customers to buy what they neither want nor need . . .

By contrast, the approach adopted in this learning programme is that selling involves a set of skills and an awareness that bridges the gap between a customer and a need. Furthermore, that selling is a service which can only be founded in a relationship based on trust and respect. The word 'Active' in the title is used to acknowledge the need of the salesperson to develop that relationship with the customer.[1]

The aims of the learning programme were also listed in the Introduction. These aims were:

1 To help you review how effective you are as a salesperson.
2 To identify and practise the skills of active selling.
3 To develop a continuing awareness that face-to-face skills are an important, though not exclusive, part of the active-selling approach adopted by Sherratt & Hughes in its service to the public.

The two key assumptions that underpinned these learning aims were also described:

1 Because selling, like any other form of relationship, is based on an interaction between two or more people, then it is important to recognize that although guidelines can be offered *it is impossible to provide a set of right answers.*
2 *That whatever your present level of knowledge and skills it is possible to develop and improve. Your own experiences provide the best guide for both what and how you need to develop.*

At the end of the programme individual members of staff were asked to reflect on any outstanding training and development needs that they had identified during the three parts. In addition, they were asked to discuss with their manager:

1 What they had learned about their skills in selling.
2 Any suggestions they may have about improving the quality of service to the customer.

The manager's brief   In the detailed brief for manager's their important role in the learning process was itemized as follows:

1 To brief all their staff about the programme.
2 To lead the training sessions.
3 To respond to the needs and queries raised under sections of the programme. (Detailed notes of guidance were included.)
4 To respond to the wider issues raised by staff on completion of the programme. (In addition to taking responsibility for both training needs and suggestions on service, managers were also required to offer feedback to staff on their 'selling skills'.)

An important part of their briefing included some guidance on the learning approach. This stated that the approach:

1 Is developmental (i.e. building on existing skills and knowledge) rather than remedial (i.e. assuming that staff have little or no skills in this area).
2 Assumes that staff can learn from reviewing and reflecting on their own experiences rather than offering or leading them to 'five golden rules'. It is a *learning* rather than a *teaching* approach.
3 Assumes that every member of staff, irrespective of length and quality of experience, can continue to learn about the process of selling.
4 Assumes that effective selling is based on a set of face-to-face skills and a need for a continuing awareness about the wider relationship between Sherratt & Hughes and potential customers.

In addition to the written brief the training officer also held meetings with the managers involved to talk them through the learning programme and to deal with any questions they raised about the detail or the process of implementation.

Comments

This programme was implemented in the spring and summer of 1989, and, like 'First service', now forms part of the induction process for new members of staff. Prior to my involvement the organization had undertaken its own analysis and diagnosis so my role was limited to designing the intervention strategy. An important part of that strategy was to build in a feedback loop to senior managers. (Each branch manager was asked to feed in the final observations from staff to group office who would then respond to the issues raised.) It was also an essential part of the strategy to involve managers in the learning process. (This also fits in with Sherratt & Hughes's view on the role and responsibility of the manager.) Unfortunately, the physical constraints (small numbers of staff in scattered locations) largely determined the nature of the strategy adopted, i.e. a learning programme facilitated by branch managers.

The positive side to this constraint, however, is that because Sherratt & Hughes is still a relatively new group much of their recent operational concerns have aimed at achieving a common image and approach in all their shops. To this end, the training strategy reinforces this aspect of their culture.

Finally, the model of relationship which underpins the 'Active selling skills' programme is based on the helping relationship described in Chapter 2.

Reference

1. I would like to thank Sherratt & Hughes for giving me permission to quote from the 'Active selling skills' programme.

6 The trainer as learner

In the previous chapters I have attempted to describe an approach to managing the process of learning and change, and have applied this approach to the respective areas of training, counselling, and consultancy. In doing so I have focused the attention on one side of the helping relationship, i.e. the learner, and have deliberately minimized any comments about the implications of this approach for the trainer. In this chapter I wish to redress the balance. In particular, I want to examine some key areas affecting the trainer in managing that relationship. These areas are:

- a code of ethics
- the training profession
- the effective trainer
- the learning process for the trainer
- the role of the trainer in the organization
- personal development

The comments that form this chapter are not only drawn from my direct experience, and the reported experiences of the many co-trainers I have worked with over the years, but also from the issues and concerns expressed by trainers that have attended programmes that I have provided. These issues and concerns, mentioned briefly in the Introduction (see p. xiv *et seq.*) I view as open-ended questions that each trainer will need to resolve for him- or herself. The following are my answers, based on my experiences, and are offered here as material to stimulate and provoke the reader into forming his or her own conclusions.

A code of ethics

In an earlier chapter (p. 30 *et seq.*), I argued that the idea of the trainer as a catalyst does not fit comfortably in the context of the helping relationship. Even in the context of the traditional relationship the possibility of a trainer operating as a neutral intermediary between the organization and the learner—neither influencing nor being influenced by the experience—is an illusion. The trainer who defines his or her role in this way, and consciously avoids the possibility of 'contaminating' the learning event by suppressing or hiding personal values and beliefs, is modelling through his or her behaviour as cogent a set of values as a trainer operating at the other end of the spectrum.

Throughout any learning event the trainer is making a multitude of choices—selecting and presenting information, designing and running experiences, responding or not responding to the needs and behaviour of the learner. Each one of these choices reflects the views, values, and beliefs of the trainer. That these choices are made implicitly rather than explicitly is also a reflection of particular beliefs. One of the dangers with the implicit approach is that the full nature of this influence is not appreciated by the trainer. One former colleague that I worked with would argue relentlessly that his role was one of neutral intermediary and that the sole function of training was to improve the profitability of the organization through increased productivity or more efficient use of resources. In his work with groups he would encourage them to focus on 'the bottom line', i.e. money. This commitment, however laudable, was never acknowledged by him to be a value judgement! More importantly, nor was he willing to acknowledge that his reiteration of that belief had a powerful influence on groups.

The fact that the trainer will inevitably 'contaminate' the learning process is not, in my judgement, a matter of regret. Rather, I believe it to be the basis of a need for a professional code of ethics, which, of itself, will do much to focus on the need to improve the quality of training provided in this country. Some of the key statements I would like to see in such a code would include the following.

1 The role of the trainer is to provide and manage learning experiences.
2 The trainer is obliged to offer clear guidelines and contracts to both learners and the sponsors of that learning event.
3 The trainer should specify in the contract both the desired outcomes of that learning (e.g. to improve knowledge and skills in influencing) and also the possible unwanted outcomes (e.g. the learner may lose confidence).
4 The relationship between the trainer and the learner must be based on total confidentiality.
5 In the event of a conflict of interest between the learner and the organization the primary responsibility of the trainer is to the learner.
6 The trainer has a responsibility to work only to the agreed contract of learning, and under no circumstances should he or she work outside that contract unless all parties have made an explicit agreement to that effect.
7 The trainer has a responsibility to work always within the limits of his or her expertise.
8 The trainer needs to recognize that he or she operates with values, beliefs and assumptions, and that these need to be acknowledged as such with the learner.
9 The trainer has a responsibility to recognize that the learner has the right to choose to learn and not to learn.
10 The trainer needs to recognize that the relationship with the learner is one of trust and privilege and that he or she has a responsibility not to abuse the learner.
11 Within these constraints the trainer has a right to exercise a professional judgement that the attendance of a learner on an event is potentially harmful to that individual or to the others attending.

While I recognize that the above may not be an exhaustive list I believe that it contains some of the more pertinent issues. In addition to contributing to the improvement of training, by providing protection to the learner, the trainer, and the organization, I also believe that the production of such a code would do much to ensure the necessary separation of training from the related area of personnel.

The training profession

When I came into training in 1975 the professionalization of the personnel function, largely through the efforts of the Institute of Personnel Management, was beginning to take effect. Although this was a necessary development for the wider personnel function it had the unfortunate effect of ensuring that the recognized qualification for a training officer was Associate Membership of IPM. In more recent years the Institute of Training and Development has offered a reputable qualification but the timing has ensured that training is still seen as one of the disciplines of personnel. Based on my experience I believe that training as a profession has a closer relationship to the disciplines of counselling, psychotherapy and education than it does to industrial relations, management services, manpower planning, and personnel administration. Whereas the former grouping has a very clear relationship with training (i.e. helping people to learn and change), the latter group has only the tenuous link of being concerned with the people side of organizations. My concern in making this point is not to advocate that training should be organizationally separate from personnel—it makes every sense to remain there—but that the responsible development of the training role will be inhibited as long as it is viewed as part of the personnel profession. One immediate effect of this subordination is that for many organizations training is too often seen as a short step in a normal career pattern. Either someone takes up the role as a precursor to a senior personnel position or as a short-stay placing in the development of the line manager. Either way, the person is unlikely to stay in post for more than five years. This leads to an impoverished view of the profession of training, and does not allow for the necessary development of skills.

Given that it takes at least two years before the post-holder can develop enough skills and understanding before he or she can provide a reasonable service, organizations are unlikely to develop the expertise required to offer the kinds of activity described in this book. Unfortunately, unless decision-makers in organizations begin to recognize that the requirements of an effective trainer far exceed the simple acquisition of limited knowledge and a few classroom skills, then there is little chance that the quality of service provided will improve.

The effective trainer

Like most people coming to the training role for the first time I very quickly developed an internalized role model of the effective trainer. This role model, to which I aspired, proved to be a composite picture of those trainers and educators who had influenced me significantly over the years. My formal development for taking on this role—a masters degree that included personnel management—provided a lot of information about the theory and practice of personnel. I was fortunate that my degree also covered organization theory and behaviour. What it did not provide, however, was any understanding or skills in being a trainer. I then studied for the Associate examination of the IPM but decided, after six months, that this had little to offer apart from the normal cachet of a professional qualification.

Having taken up a training post I quickly attended a number of programmes which professed to offer such skills. In spite of these programmes the only guidance I had to carry out my tasks was the role model in my head. This model—which I shall refer to as 'Supertrainer'—represented all that seemed best in practice, approach, and methodology. My 'Supertrainer' was characterized by:

- a remarkable capacity to present theory in a way that made immediate sense;
- an ability to make learning both enjoyable and significant;
- an ability to discriminate between the different needs and comfort levels of individuals;
- an appreciable level of self-confidence that always fell short of arrogance;
- an ability to cope with whatever occurred on the learning event.

Not only did I aspire to this role model but I also believed, however fleetingly, that I already possessed all these qualities and abilities. Unfortunately, more frequently I also believed that one day I would discover that I possessed none. This internal vacillation produced huge swings in my confidence level, and, irrespective of my highs and lows, was part of a wider process of debilitation. Because, while I was monitoring my performance in this way, my self-consciousness was a distraction from being aware of myself and the group. The result of this distraction was a failure to pick up the needs of individuals and a failure to recognize that my emotional responses to groups and individuals were subsumed by my concerns about performing. Nor, till many years later, did I begin to question the nature of 'Supertrainer'.

The whole foundation of 'Supertrainer' was questionable at many levels. First, it was a model based on my responses to individuals, and did not recognize that other people in the same learning event had many different judgements about the trainers concerned. Second, I did not recognize that I had screened out other aspects of the trainers that did not fit my overall judgement. Third, it was a model based on *observation*: I interpreted what I saw and had no knowledge of what these trainers experienced. What I believed to be signs of confidence could in reality have been symptoms of defensiveness, distance, or insouciance. The gulf between the way I saw others perform and the way that I felt when undertaking similar tasks became a source of increasing dissatisfaction. As I became more dissatisfied my anxiety level would increase, and the more I then attempted to disguise or hide my anxiety. The result was that my anxiety kept feeding on itself. Having originally approached the job on the basis that all I really required was some basic theory and a few classroom skills then my dissatisfaction and anxiety levels could only result from my inadequacy. It was only years later—*when I felt safe enough to talk to other trainers about their experiences*—that I began to realize that the problem might owe more to the distinguishing characteristics of the job than it did to any inherent personal deficiencies.

The characteristics of the job itself—which neither my role model nor my education and training prepared me for—generate a certain level of stress. These characteristics are as follows.

1 Each week or programme most trainers have to take responsibility for developing relationships not only with a new group, *but must also take responsibility for facilitating effective relationships within groups.*
2 The trainer is one of the few professionals whose performance is publicly evaluated on a weekly basis.
3 The trainer also knows—whatever format is being used—that the evaluation is fundamentally concerned with judgements about the *kind* of person he or she is, and how he or she manages relationships.
4 The degree of uncertainty can also be highly demanding. (For example, learning how to cope with groups who are struggling with counter-dependency, see p. 50)

All these characteristics create 'performance anxiety' for trainers; and those who are new to the job, or who habitually attempt to distance themselves from their own emotions, are likely to experience what has been described as 'burn-out'.[1] This term, which has been used widely in the helping professions over the last decade, describes the physical, mental, and emotional exhaustion which arises when the helper does not effectively manage him- or herself. Although burn-out can manifest itself in dramatic terms (e.g. an outpouring of emotions to learners or colleagues, a hasty decision to leave training etc.), it is usually accumulated over a period of time. Some of the symptoms associated with burn-out are:

• Tiredness	Excessive tiredness at the end of the day, or week, which is exacerbated by an inability to sleep.
• Illness	A number of minor illnesses (e.g. colds, 'flu, aches and pains etc.) which are difficult to shake off; or a serious stress-related illness.
• Not coping	Difficulties in coping with daily routines (e.g. administration, preparing for programmes etc.), and accumulating a list of unfinished tasks.
• Emotional see-saw	General emotional instability which involves frequent and rapid movement between extremes, e.g. depression—elation—depression etc.
• Over-indulgence	An over-indulgence in any number of activities, e.g. smoking, drinking, eating.
• Punishing	Over-compensating for tiredness and an inability to cope by punishing individuals and groups.
• Avoiding all conflict	Denying, avoiding, or suppressing all manifestations of conflict.

In terms of guarding against, or dealing with, burn-out there are a number of both general guidelines and specific actions to undertake when working. As to the *general guidelines* these could include:

- Physical fitness

  Because of the training environment (hotels and training centres) it is relatively easy for the trainer to lose a reasonable level of physical fitness required to remain effective. The adoption of an appropriate regime of exercise and healthy diet is an essential requirement.

- Personal development

  Being involved in learning events requires a continuing need to develop self-awareness and skills. Without this development the trainer is likely to become less effective (see later in this chapter).

- External support

  The trainer working in the organization can end up feeling isolated. Where no immediate support is available the trainer will need to develop an external network. The type of support required may well include: (1) time to talk through experiences of a learning event, (2) someone willing to listen to your concerns and to offer you feedback, (3) counselling.

- Workload

  It is important to provide time to recover from different learning experiences, and this time should be recognized as part of the normal workload.

Within these general guidelines there are some *specific actions* that the trainer can take while involved in running a learning event. These actions are:

- Self-acceptance

  The trainer needs to have a clear picture of his or her abilities and should avoid the self-imposed impossible demands, e.g. to be perfect, to ensure that everyone on the programme learns everything and enjoys themselves etc. The trainer who cannot accept him- or herself will invariably end up putting pressure on the learner to be different. This will then generate more pressure for the trainer when the learner begins to resist.

- Mutual support

  When working with co-trainers there is a need to have meetings out of session in order to: (1) talk about the event, (2) clarify objectives and approach, (3) give and receive feedback. These meetings need to be effectively 'policed', however, because they can drain energy from all parties (see later section on co-training).

- Anxiety

  At moments of anxiety and stress there is often an interruption of the breathing (light rapid breathing, swallowing, restricted breathing, for example). At such moments taking a few deep breaths makes it easier to cope with the cause of the anxiety.

- Physical support

  For similar reasons the trainer should pay

attention to the need for physical support.
When sitting, ensure that the body is evenly
supported across all points of contact with the
chair. When standing, ensure that the posture
is evenly balanced and that the soles of the
feet are firmly on the ground.

- Clear boundaries

The trainer needs to have a clear line of distinction between who he or she is and who the
other person is. Confusion of the boundaries is
always likely to arise in the helping relationship because of the process of projection (see
pp. 10–11). When the boundary is eroded the
trainer will end up: (1) becoming locked into
the learner's pattern of behaviour, (2) taking
too much responsibility for the learning,
(3) falling into old patterns of compulsive
behaviour, e.g. going too fast, not listening etc.

- Finishing business

Because the trainer is involved in starting and
finishing so many new relationships it is very
easy for him or her to carry away regrets or
concerns about what occurred. ('If only I had
said . . .'.) These omissions may include:
unexpressed emotions or feedback, a failure to
clarify a communication problem, an
unresolved conflict. Such omissions are then
carried by the trainer into the next group with
the increasing danger that more is accumulated.

- Feedback

When receiving negative feedback, either during
or at the end of events the trainer's response
should be a *thinking* and not a *feeling* one. He
or she needs to listen carefully and extract
from what is offered ideas which can be used
on future occasions. By contrast, the trainer
should respond in both ways to positive feedback. The trainer who can enjoy being appreciated is more likely to offer appreciations to
others.

The learning process for the trainer

One of the reasons for the deficiencies of my model of 'Supertrainer'
was an assumption that it represented a finished product, i.e. at some
stage in the future I would achieve that state of excellence. The time
involved in the transition might take months or years, but at some
indefinite point I would arrive at completion. What I did not realize was
that there is no end—learning and change simply continue. The
anxieties and concerns I had sixteen years ago are the same ones I still
have to deal with now. What has changed, however, is my response to
them and the realization that knowledge and skills are far less important
than the simple ability to be able to talk *with* people as a person and not
as a trainer, consultant, or counsellor.

Learning for me has involved discarding many areas that I used to consider to be of fundamental importance. At one level I have found it necessary to discard:

- a desire to have a complete understanding of X's theory, and how it relates to the theory of Y and Z;
- what a trainer *should* do and what he or she *should not* do;
- all generalized statements about the role of the trainer.

At another level I have found it necessary to discard:

- any desire to make my sense of well-being dependent on the judgement of others;
- any desire to prove myself to others or myself;
- any wish to judge myself in relation to the performances of others;
- any desire to pretend that I know the answer, particularly when pressed by someone to offer my view.

What I have replaced these old patterns with is a willingness to trust both myself and the learner to arrive at the solution. The source of these changes has been the feedback that I have received both as a trainer and a learner. The process of learning and change has at times been painful, difficult, joyous and liberating.

Learning has often been difficult to achieve when I have been a member of a closed group of trainers, i.e. a group of trainers who have worked exclusively together for a period of time. Such groupings tend to develop a particular culture and norms of behaviour which ultimately work against the needs of individuals within the group. What compounds the problems that any closed group experiences is that trainers assume that their collective expertise provides sufficient safeguards against the dangers. In reality, however, that expertise can become a weapon for punishment for self and others, e.g. playing psychological games of one-upmanship. Groups of trainers who aim at self-sufficiency in managing the problems that invariably rise will ultimately reduce the effectiveness of both the group and individual members in the group. What is required in these circumstances is (1) the use of an outside facilitator to run team-building events (on average at least once a year); (2) members of the group to seek every opportunity to co-train with people from outside the group; and (3) for members of that group to undertake personal development activities with other organizations and reputable bodies. Only under extreme circumstances should members offer regular counselling to each other on personal or professional issues. Hence, my earlier comment in this chapter about the need for co-trainers to 'police' their meetings, not least to ensure that only issues of immediate business priority are dealt with.

As a contrast to the problems that arise from situations of exclusiveness, the trainer is also likely to experience problems in the context of his or her home life. Partly this is due to the particular characteristics of the job—being away from home, late nights etc.—but also because the continuing process of learning and change puts a great strain on the relationship with the partner. Committed trainers are those who are open to learning about who they are and what they want. In discovering this information and responding to it trainers are unlikely to be aware how threatening this can be to their partners. Even when their partners are engaged in a similar career the increasing dissonance between their respective paths of learning and change require both parties to spend time managing the relationship. The worst option is to simply assume that there will be no such problem in the relationship.

The role of the trainer in the organization

Another problem area that the trainer will have to deal with is the inevitable conflict stemming from his or her role as an agent of change in the organization. The traditional view of the role of the trainer in the organization assumes that there is no inherent conflict. Central to this view is the notion that the organization determines what is required in terms of appropriate knowledge, skills, and attitudes, and that the trainer—working within that brief—simply makes a contribution to achieving the specified goals. The only problem with this particular view is that in practice it does not happen.

First, it assumes an incredible clarity of vision and planning by senior management in organizations. If such clarity exists then the vast majority of practising trainers are excluded from sharing the vision. At best the trainer may be told/instructed/invited to run a particular learning event on, say, communications skills or new technology. Second, even when a need is specified clearly, the possibility that it represents the best use of resources—in dealing with the immediate problem or of its being a priority need—is often questionable. Third, it assumes that the outcomes of learning events can be specified and delivered with the same degree of certainty as can be applied, say, to the manufacture of sausages. For example, I was asked to run a course on assertiveness by a manager who had diagnosed that his staff were too dependent and passive. Four days after the completion of the course the manager rang me to complain that his staff were now questioning his instructions and judgements. During the course of our discussion about the programme and its outcomes, he said, 'I didn't want them to be assertive in that kind of way'. (This conversation took place in spite of having a clear contract which suggested that such behaviours were likely outcomes.)

My intention in making these points is not to be critical of senior management but rather to criticize the poverty of the traditional view of training. The basic role of the trainer is to change people and organizations. The nature of that change can not be specified by senior managers or trainers but will be determined by the interaction between the trainer and the learner. A dramatic illustration of this view can be derived from the experiences of many organizations who have undertaken race-awareness training. The objective of such training is to develop positive attitudes to racial differences. The outcomes of such training, however, suggest that a significant number of delegates have left such programmes with even more entrenched negative views. This difference between goals and outcomes, immediately obvious in this example, is also true of all kinds of training (see similar example, pp. 2–3).

Because of all the above reasons the role of the trainer in the organization is often ambiguous. Trainers who wait for a clear brief, and who set themselves the task of carrying out that brief will discover that the service they provide will be of little benefit to the organization. By contrast, trainers who accept the ambiguity and seek to develop a *proactive*, as opposed to a *reactive*, role are more likely to address the real needs of the organization. In choosing this path, however, they will be attempting to influence the nature and direction of change of the organization. This will involve questioning and challenging the views and behaviour of everyone in the organization, from managing director downwards. It will also involve offering a point of view that may be accepted, rejected, or modified by decision-makers. Managing this role—without losing credibility, influence or the job!—is probably the major challenge facing any trainer working within or for the organization. The trainer who errs too far on the side of caution is likely to have a negligible impact on the organization. The trainer who goes to the other extreme could easily be marginalized or lose his or her job.

The reason I pose the dilemma in such extreme terms is simply to recognize that whatever difficulties are posed by attempting to manage change in individuals, such difficulties take on a different order of magnitude at the organizational level. The resistances that can be deployed by an individual (see pp. 32–37) have the function of protecting him or her from injury: the resistances deployed by organizations have the function of protecting the powerful from giving up that power.

Organizations exist within a particular society and their nature and power structure reflect that which exists in the wider arena. Despite all the legislation and the changes in social attitudes over the last twenty years people in positions of power are still dominantly white, middle-aged, middle-class men. There have been significant attempts to change recruitment practices in recent years, but, in spite of these changes, organizations are still controlled and managed by members of this elite. If you doubt this statement, simply look at the distribution and numbers of women and members of the ethnic communities within the hierarchy of your own organization. The fact that your organization may have a clear equal opportunities policy does not in itself guarantee change. In fact, the adoption of such a policy may be the extent of the change. One of the paradoxes of the present situation is that the nature and pace of change, in these terms, are being managed by those who have the most to lose if the change was fully effected. As history has demonstrated many times, the capacity of any ruling class to give up power voluntarily is not one to instil hope in the powerless.

Apart from having the power the elite also have a major influence on determining the culture of the organization. The culture most clearly associated with white, middle-aged, middle-class males in organizations is one which embraces the following values.

- The task will always take precedence over the people.
- Competition is 'instinctive' and healthy.
- Work is more important than home life.
- Work is serious and means producing 'things' (e.g. products, reports, balance sheets, etc.).
- Employees need to be controlled and directed.

- People will do the minimum work for the maximum reward.
- To succeed you need to be determined and tough.
- Demonstrating to others that you work hard is important (particularly if you are a senior manager).

I appreciate that, like any generalization, the above is not applicable to all members of all organizations. I am also aware, however, that in the last ten years particularly these values have been more clearly stated by senior managers as regrettable facts of life.

Any trainer will realize from experience that the consequences of living by these values is that people suffer. Even the 'winners' in such a system pay a price (e.g. stress, overwork, self-doubt etc.), while the 'losers' pay an even bigger price (e.g. despair, a sense of failure or impotence). In choosing to play safe the trainer will either end up supporting these values or helping people to develop coping mechanisms for survival. The trainer, by contrast, who recognizes that these values are inimical to personal growth and change will discover that his or her role will inevitably lead to conflict with the decision-makers. This is not to imply either that the trainer is the only source of wisdom or insight into the processes of the organization, or that the role he or she should undertake is to subvert the culture. Such a view is both arrogant and destructive for all parties. What it does mean, however, is that in all aspects of the role (training, consultancy, counselling) the trainer needs continually to question the purpose and outcomes of any learning event. To what extent does this event, and the trainer's contribution, support or question the prevailing culture?

Because the trainer has a place in the authority structure of the organization—often a fairly lowly one—the only resources he or she will be able to draw on are the ability to influence. Too often, in my experience, trainers view this task in pessimistic terms. The basis of such pessimism seems to stem from a mixture of bad experiences with individual managers and from self-doubt about their perceived credibility within the organization. The reality, however, is that the capacity to influence is much greater than we realize. Not least because even the most reactionary authority figure in the organization has some concern or dissatisfaction with the nature of the organization. (In fact, it would often appear that there is a direct correlation between the degree of authoritarianism and the level of dissatisfaction.) The trainer only needs to create the opportunity to talk with senior managers and to have the patience to truly listen and wait, and the chance to intervene will be presented.

Dealing with organizational resistance involves the same skills as dealing with that of the learner (see p. 32 *et seq.*). In the same way that attempts to push individuals through the point of resistance merely increase the behaviour, so do organizations react when the trainer pushes against the culture and the power structure of the organization. A more helpful strategy is to empower individuals and teams so that they can consciously create the kind of organization that they wish to have. The views and values of the trainer—which should be shared explicitly—are of no more, or less, importance than any other member of the organization. The trainer's capacity to influence and be influenced by others from a position of equality is, in my judgement, the major skill that needs to be developed.

Personal development

If for no other reasons than the various vicissitudes and pressures mentioned above, there is a continuing need for personal development. Simply by providing a service within an organization the trainer will discover that the combined effects of managing learning events and the role will generate more questions than answers. The first area of questions will concern the approach and methodology currently employed. (These may be designated 'technical' concerns.) The second area will be to do with personal issues, and will arise from feedback received and awareness of behaviour (i.e. what he or she finds easy or difficult to accomplish). The extent to which the answers can be found within the organization is very limited, and the trainer will need to look elsewhere for personal development. Even in organizations which have a large training establishment and many experienced trainers, these limitations still exist. Those organizations which have a healthy approach to training recognize these limitations and are willing to send their staff to external bodies, or bring in consultants, to meet their needs.

There are many established resources that provide personal development programmes for trainers—particularly if the trainer is willing to consider the contribution of psychotherapy in this arena—and I have no intention of making specific recommendations of appropriate bodies. What I would like to do, however, is to offer some specific guidelines for making that choice. The cost of personal development can be very high, and, in my experience, the quality can be extremely variable. The following guidelines can be applied to any provider—management college, training or therapy institute, growth centre—and the more reputable the institution the more willing it will be to meet your request for information.

The first step in planning a development activity is to identify the need(s). What problem are you trying to cope with, or what skill are you attempting to develop? When I run workshops for trainers I ask them to complete a *self-assessment checklist* (see Figure 6.1). The purpose of the exercise is to help trainers identify particular skills that they wanted to examine and develop on the programme. It is not offered as an exhaustive list of all the skills, and should be seen very much as a starting-point to provide detail for individuals needs. The reader who would like to use this exercise is asked to make an immediate OK–*not* OK decision for each item and then to make detailed notes in the column provided. Not all the items on the checklist are mutually exclusive.

Skill	OK	Not OK	Comment
1 Handling 'difficult' course members			
2 Managing the balance between involvement and detachment, i.e. how close you get to learners			
3 Coping with negative feedback			
4 Developing effective relationships with colleagues			
5 Managing feedback activities			
6 Confronting without punishing			
7 Showing caring			
8 Not confusing assertion with aggression			
9 Taking care of your own needs, interests, concerns			
10 Managing own feelings			
11 Using intuition			
12 Dealing with aggression from others			
13 Handling difficult groups			
14 Being willing to experiment with interventions			
15 Sharing feelings with groups			
16 Allowing individuals/ groups to manage their own learning			
17 Being aware of own limits/competence			
18 Knowing how you can be 'wound up' by others			
19 Dealing with own anxiety			
20 Asking for help			
21 Offering support			
22 Handling win/lose competition			
23 Handling diversions			
24 Listening to the 'content' of what is said, and the 'process' of how it is said			
25 Managing uncertainty			
26 Creativity in responding to the needs of groups/ individuals			

Figure 6.1 *Self-assessment checklist*

Having answered these questions you will find it useful to talk over your findings with a colleague.

Having clearly established the need(s) the trainer should contact the consultant/therapist/institute with a view to assessing their ability to provide a service. If you have no first-hand experience of the provider, ask to talk to the person involved in running the programme. If that person says that the programme will meet your needs ask them: (1) the learning method used, (2) the person's experience and qualifications for running the programme, (3) the names and telephone numbers of previous users that you can contact, and (4) for them to send you details of the programme. In making this request of well-established institutions *do not be deterred by the fact that they may well have a good reputation in providing this service*. Often large institutions unjustifiably trade on a historical reputation which is no longer deserved. By contrast, anyone currently providing a professional service will be more than willing to meet your requests. Whenever possible ask to meet the person, as opposed to having a telephone conversation. This is particularly important when you are considering either a high-risk programme or a long-term commitment. As well as receiving professional information you will be able to make important personal judgements about the person you are dealing with. Many of the therapy institutes provide short 'taster' events to enable learners to reach these decisions. Similarly, some management colleges provide 'open days' which meet the same need.

This need for caution is particularly evident when the trainer considers approaching growth centres or therapists to provide development needs. At the moment there is no system of certification or licensing to control providers (though this will be rectified in 1992 under the terms of the Single Market), so the quality of service can be very poor. One of the marketing ploys that therapists use on their literature which can be very misleading is the claim that they have 'trained with X or the Institute Y'. Such a statement often means that the individual has merely attended a learning event provided by that person or institute and does not mean that they have been certified to practise. If you have any doubt about such claims ask to see the appropriate certificate. If you consider one-to-one therapy, as opposed to the group format, it is important to agree a clear contract at the start about the number and frequency of the one-hour sessions involved. Listen to the therapist's recommendation, and then decide on your initial commitment. (Personally, I would commit myself to no more than five sessions with a therapist that I have never worked with before.) The reasons for advocating such a cautious approach are twofold. One, it is very easy to become over-dependent on the therapist, and that is not a good position to be in when making sound judgements about the length and cost of your personal development. Two, therapists have an obvious commercial interest in developing a long-term relationship.

It is very important to trust your intuition and common sense when choosing a therapist. The most important criterion in this respect is your willingness to trust their response to you when you are feeling vulnerable. For anyone considering this area for the first time I would recommend that you read *'In Our Own Hands: A Book of Self-Help Therapy* by Sheila

Ernst and Lucy Goodison.[2] Although the book is specifically addressed to women it provides descriptions of the different approaches available, and offers some very useful guidelines on how to proceed.

Planning personal development checklist
1 What are my needs? (self-assessment and/or feedback)
2 What services are currently available?
3 Collect written information about programmes.
4 Talk to the trainer/therapist in person.
5 Ask for details of qualifications and experience.
6 Attend any introductory session or programme.
7 Where appropriate, agree a limited contract.
8 If therapist/trainer does not meet your needs end the contract.

I realize, in closing this chapter, I have focused on some of the important problems that the trainer encounters in attempting to manage learning and change in others. Having done so, I do not want to neglect the many pleasures and benefits that are also available. Those of us who enjoy being with others when they discover new opportunities and different approaches to dealing with problems recognize that we have a privileged role in organizational life. I am also aware that the effects of our work, both good and bad, go much wider.

Finally, to all the people I have worked with—as learner, client, co-trainer, colleague, friend—I wish to thank you for all the pleasures that I have enjoyed.

Summary

In this final chapter I have looked at some of the issues that affect the trainer who seeks to offer a helping relationship to learners. I have argued that the relatively low status of the training profession has seriously impeded the development of an effective service to organizations. At this time the responsibility for improvement rests on the committed trainer planning and implementing a personal development strategy. To assist the trainer I have offered some guidelines on how this could be managed.

References

1. Cary Cherniss, *Staff Burnout: Job Stress in the Human Services* (Sage Publications, California, 1980).
2. Sheila Ernst and Lucy Goodison *In Our Own Hands: A Book of Self-help Therapy* (Women's Press, 1981).

Further reading

Gestalt Herman, Stanley M. and Korenich, Michael, *Authentic Management: A Gestalt Orientation to Organisations and Their Development* (Addison-Wesley, 1977).
Describes some of the Gestalt concepts and relates them to issues in organizational life. Also contains exercises, case studies and identifies key issues in the consultancy process.
Perls, Fritz, *The Gestalt Approach and Eyewitness to Therapy* (Bantam, 1976).
Two books in one volume. The first is a readable introduction to Gestalt theory; the second contains transcripts of training films.
Polster, Erving and Polster, Miriam, *Gestalt Therapy Integrated: Contours of Theory and Practise* (Vintage Books, New York, 1974).
Good introduction to the theory with a brief outline of some training techniques.
Simkin, James, *Gestalt Therapy Mini Lectures* (Celestial Arts, California, 1971).
Very readable book, particularly useful for the trainer. Looks at theoretical and practical issues.
The Gestalt Journal.
Published twice a year by the Center for Gestalt Development Inc. Vol. 1 (1978–). Address:
The Gestalt Journal
PO Box 990
Highland
New York
USA 12528

Training Adair, John *et al.*, *A Handbook of Management Training Exercises*, 2 vols (BACIE, 1980–82).
Vol. 1 contains 25 exercises with background notes; Vol. 2 contains references to the background notes.
Biddle, Derek and Evenden, Robin, *Human Aspects of Management* (IPM, 1980)
Useful sourcebook for trainers, containing theory and exercises on management style, managing change, conflict, communication etc.
Bion, W.R., *Experiences in Groups* (Tavistock, 1968).
The Tavistock approach to groups.
Brandes, Donna and Phillips, Howard, *'Gamesters' Handbook* (Hutchinson, 1978).
Source for training exercises.
Phillips, Keri and Fraser, Tony, *The Management of Interpersonal Skills Training* (Gower, 1982).
Deals with design issues, managing groups, feedback, and evaluation.
Shaffer, John B.P. and Galinsky, M. David, *Models of Group Therapy and Sensitivity Training* (Prentice Hall, 1974).
Lengthy descriptions of the different approaches.

Counselling

Biestek, Felix P., *The Casework Relationship* (Allen & Unwin, 1961).
Seven broad principles of counselling are discussed, e.g. acceptance, confidentiality etc.

Egan, Gerard, *The Skilled Helper: Models, Skills, and Methods for Effective Helping*, 2nd edn (Brooks/Cole, California, 1982).
Presents overview model of counselling which comprises three stages: exploration, goal-setting, action.

Munro, E.A., Manthei, R.J. and Small, J.J., *Counselling: A Skills Approach*, 2nd edn (Metheun, 1983).
Simple and clear introduction to counselling.

Passons, William R., *Gestalt Approaches in Counselling* (Holt, Rhinehart & Winston, 1975).
Includes model of counselling, theory, but concentrates on awareness, language, non-verbal behaviour as sources for the counsellor.

Consultancy

Beckhard, Richard, 'The Confrontation Meeting', in *Harvard Business Review*, 45, No. 2 (1967), 149–55.

Bennis, Warren G., 'Changing Organisations', in *The Journal of Applied Behavioural Sciences*, Vol. 2, No. 3 (1966), 247–63.

Perrow, Charles, *Complex Organisations: A Critical Essay* (Scott, Foresman and Co., 1972).
View of the major perspectives on organizations, including the human relations model.

Pugh, D.S., *Organisation Theory* (Penguin, 1979).
Companion volume to *Writers on Organisations* by D.S. Pugh, *et al.*

Walton, Richard E., *Confrontations and Third Party Consultation* (Addison-Wesley, 1969).
Primarily concerned with the management of interpersonal conflict as an OD intervention.

Personal development

Dychtwald, Ken, *Body-Mind* (Jove, 1978)
Concerned with developing body-mind awareness, and illustrates how the physical self mirrors the shape and scope of the mind.

Joy, W. Brugh, *Joy's Way: A Map for the Transformational Journey* (J.P. Tarcher Inc., Los Angeles, 1979).
Perspective on the nature of personal issues and how they can be experienced as transformations.

Kovel, Joel, *A Complete Guide to Therapy* (Pelican, 1976).
Comprehensive review of the major therapies.

Madders, Jane, *Stress and Relaxation*, 3rd edn (Martin Dunitz, 1981).
Techniques of natural relaxation intended to reduce stress in everyday life. Exercises can obviously be introduced into appropriate training programmes.

Sheehy, Gail, *Passages: Predictable Crises of Adult LIfe* (Bantam Books, 1976).
Descriptions of crises and life patterns.

Index